A Biography of the Spirit

A Biography of the Spirit

"There lies the dearest freshness deep down things"

CREED p184

by

John C. Haughey

ORBIS BOOKS
Maryknoll, New York 10545

ORBIS ✪ BOOKS
Maryknoll, New York 10545

Fathers and Brothers
MARYKNOLL™

Founded in 1970, Orbis Books endeavors to publish works that enlighten the mind, nourish the spirit, and challenge the conscience. The publishing arm of the Maryknoll Fathers and Brothers, Orbis seeks to explore the global dimensions of the Christian faith and mission, to invite dialogue with diverse cultures and religious traditions, and to serve the cause of reconciliation and peace. The books published reflect the views of their authors and do not represent the official position of the Maryknoll Society. To learn more about Maryknoll and Orbis Books, please visit our website at www.maryknollsociety.org.

Copyright © 2015 by John C. Haughey

Published by Orbis Books, Maryknoll, New York 10545-0302.

Manufactured in the United States of America.

Library of Congress Cataloging-in-Publication Data

Haughey, John C.
    A biography of the spirit : there lies the dearest freshness deep down things / by John C. Haughey.
        pages cm
    ISBN 978-1-62698-122-5 (pbk.)
    1. Nature—Religious aspects—Christianity—Meditations.
I. Title.
BT695.5.H375 2015
231.7—dc23

                                                            2014031615

Introduction

Why a biography of the Spirit? Why isn't there one already of the Holy Spirit, and more than one? A biography is composed of the data of a life. Since the Spirit is "the Lord and Giver of Life," according to the ancient Christian Creed, the data available must be torrential. Further, this same Christian faith has believed that the Spirit is a Person, and since biographies are done of persons, why hasn't it been done before? Probably because believers have always deferred to the second Divine Person to carry the water of such a biography of God. God Incarnate lends Itself to such depictions. But the Spirit was sent with a mission and has been carrying out this mission, not just since Pentecost but ever since there was life—if the Spirit is "the Giver of Life." So such a biography is long overdue.

This biography is going to be less focused on the testimony about the Spirit given by holy humans and more focused on the data of nature and science, which are rich sources of biographical data about the Spirit. Such a focus makes the biographical data both more voluminous and at the same time much more specific. I think the Spirit can supply a fuller intelligibility about the biota and a-biota that the sciences are pursuing.

If I were a scientist, I would not have the audacity to use the scientific data I will use in this work since each of the slivers of science through which this biography will be constructed is so specialized. But I am not a scientist, so although I am informed, I am not immersed in the findings of any particular scientific discipline. I formally confess my superficiality in matters of science and at the same time acknowledge my debt to the work of so many scientists in so many fields of study who are unearthing more and more information about the mysteries of nature. As the text will show, my sense is that their work is able to tell us more, not only about nature but also about the Spirit and how the Spirit goes about executing Its mission.

Notice the pronoun—Its! What to call the Spirit pronounly? My preference is not Him or Her because as the Lord of all that lives, the Spirit doesn't seem gendered. Just as the Spirit is trans-species-ed or supra-species-ied, so also is It supra-gendered. I think of Hopkins's poem "God's Grandeur" in this regard. Hopkins notices that "nature is never spent" and that "there lives the dearest freshness deep down things" and traces everything to the Holy Ghost, "who is bent over the world with the life which it breeds with warm breast and ah! Bright wings." This is certainly less masculine than "Lord," but there is much more to the life of the Spirit than the metaphor of a hen can convey.

If all of this seems too far out, let me say what this biography is not going to be and then let the reader decide whether to proceed. Although there are Three Persons in One God, a biography of God would make the subject matter far too complex. This is a biography about one Divine Person. If Christians have been correct for all these centuries believing that the Spirit is a person, who has a distinct mission, then a biography shouldn't seem preposterous.

Three things this will not be about: it is not going to be a theology of nature; it is not going to be a work in apologetics; it is not going to be an exhortation to be ecologically ethical. It will have accomplished what it is intended to be if it gives the reader a better sense that the Spirit is a Person with a distinct personality and is being effective in carrying out the mission for which It has been sent.

Mother Nature is a major source of this biography. But you have to piece it together one sliver at a time because there is so much to nature. And juxtaposing the slivers until a face begins to appear is not an assured undertaking, especially for the impatient. Though the face promises to be holy and awesome, and divine no less, its visibility requires some input from the observer—like, faith, hope, love.

What is the difference between what I am doing and a theology of creation? A theology of creation theologizes about creation, about created things. Things are looked at in a theological light or given a theological status. I am interested in the reverse, in what might be said about the Holy Spirit in light of what is coming to be known about things through nature and the sciences. A huge amount of attention has been given to finding out what can be known scientifically, whereas virtually no thought has been given to what scientific findings might say about God, and about the Holy Spirit in particular.

There are some presumptions behind this endeavor. One is the belief that the reality that we are able to know is one, and that this one reality is accessible to us through our senses and intelligence, including the vast amount of knowledge that specialists with like endowment have acquired and are acquiring. The second is that the more we know about nature or the world or the sciences, the more this knowledge should invite us to know more about God. To know about God through credible witnesses and traditions and the sciences invites an effort at personal integration.

The key insight that this whole volume will unpack comes from a fourth-century theologian, Basil of Caesarea. His insight was: "The Spirit completes the divine and blessed Trinity." This cannot mean there ever was an incomplete Trinity or God. It must mean that completion is what the Spirit does. The Spirit completes God immanently. So when God as Creator launches the creation, the creation will reflect that same attribute of completion. What begins immanently, in other words, shows up in the "economic" order God has made and makes.

The traditional way of describing the Spirit economically has been Sanctifier. The problem with this description is that it has become too anthropomorphized. The Spirit sanctifies "men." That leaves out everything else the Spirit is at work doing. Sanctifier has the ignorance of anthropocentrism in it. It makes the rest of creation merely an onlooker and a tool of the work of sanctification of human beings. Basil's insight brings about a different attitude about the work of the Spirit. The Spirit is the Completer. The Spirit's work is universal, a whole-making work. The stuff God makes makes itself with the help of the Completer who works through what each thing is to become complete. The teleology of the work of the Spirit is a communion of all completed things in God.

Obviously, much of creation goes off the tracks. This is where Jesus comes in. His redeeming act puts creation back on track toward communion. The work of the Spirit as Completer is most evident in the life, death, and resurrection of Jesus of Nazareth.

To take one example, the most recent scientific experiments in the brain keep on delving into the marvelous complexity of how the brain works and how its circuitry stays on track. The 2010 Human Connectome Project can be a revelation of the work of the Spirit even before human intentionality kicks in. As we are finding out, the 100,000 miles of fiber in the adult human brain, which yesterday we simply called white matter, today we can see as the circuitry that is foundational to producing all words, ideas, meaning, intelligibility—this book, for example. Does the connectivity within this 100,000-mile journey explain itself? The bias of this volume is that every increment of empirical evidence needs the complement of pneumatology to make complete sense.

The Spirit's mission, which is life, includes more than human life. The Holy Spirit doesn't become any less holy by our deepening our insight into the universality of Its work.

Insofar as the Spirit has its way in creation, death will be no more, "and the lion will lie down with the lamb. . . . There will be no ruin [or incompletion] on all my holy mountain" (Isa. 11:6–9).

The procedure I will use in this biography: each entry will begin with something I have observed in nature or learned about from one of the natural sciences or sometimes with something that occurs to me about Spirit. Then I will bring whatever theological competence I can bring to bear on one of these areas. I will propose an understanding of it in terms of how it might enlighten us about the Spirit. So an observation of nature or a finding of science, examined in the light of faith should have something to say about the Lord and Giver of Life and its Completer! And I will do this in diary form, although that will be something of an affectation because I don't think as clearly on a given day as the text would make the reader think.

April 2

Yesterday I took a walk and passed by a huge bush and heard what sounded like a hundred birds chirping excitedly. I couldn't see them very well since the bush was so leafy. A stray evictee would dart out and then straight back into whatever it was in there that was making them all so noisy. The energy of their chirping was amazing. It made me think that they were signaling their incompleteness . . . not sure whether it was for food or for mating or for a spot to sleep on for the night that was making them so querulous—Who knows? Whichever, they were about their business and had to be. I was too.

The scene stopped me in my tracks. The burst of life was enchanting. Even the tree/bush seemed to be enjoying the sport of the birds. I thought of the tree, its parents which gave it life, and I imagined the generations even before them. Yes, of course, there is the biochemical side to it and a biological side to it and all the other scientific sides to it, but foundationally there is life here. The same with the birds. Yes, there are the neurons and the talons and the photons and so on, but foundationally there is life here. The tree has its script. The birds each had their parents and their scripts. But script doesn't explain life nor do parents. They did not burst into being by spontaneous combustion. Both their history and their continuance into now are marvels to be savored. It is obtuse to take living for granted, mine and theirs, and ours!

My attention moved on. I began to see that the meaning of both me and of this flora and fauna go together. A song played in my mind: "His eye is on the sparrow, and I know he watches me." But it isn't "His" eye that I am thinking of but mine. The lens with which I view this scene is not just physiological; it also is a faith one. I haven't been told to. It's just natural. But if it is natural, why wouldn't everyone be able to see this stuff in a faith light? Even though I have been socialized into this way of seeing, I am also fully aware that I am freely doing this. It seems like I can't just let it be; I have to enchant it with faith. Where does the energy come from to do this? Why not just let it be itself?

Although I intend to let everything I look at in this book be itself, I will also try to find God in it. The cognitive energy for going this extra mile comes from having been baptized "in the name of the Father and of the Son and of the Holy Spirit." From this sacrament three theological virtues were received by me: faith, hope, and love. I don't have a better explanation for the energy than these baptismal virtues. Especially love; why do I love what I can't see, and a Who I haven't met? And hope with all my heart for something deeper than is within the range my senses deliver?

April 3

The same faith that has taught me the baptism story has also taught me that the Father and the Son have sent the Spirit and that the Spirit is on mission to make reality meaningful and to make the faith story personal, my story. And it has become so, even though I am continually weighing its cogency and measuring the rest of reality over against faith. And it's not just solitary me dreaming up this stuff. My friends have a similar way of understanding their faith, as my family had when I was younger. And the communities of worship I am part of now continue to reinforce this same understanding. We're in this narratival séance together, and we stoke each other's imaginations with the same tall tale that it is. We feed off each others' faith energies not only because we have been socialized into it but also because the story keeps giving meaning and making sense. Apart from the story—non-sense.

Fresh is the point. Each act of consciousness is a new moment for coming into being and maybe meaning. Even when the moments are dire, this faith story keeps making sense and brings further insight into both it and the self and us. I can't think of a better explanation of how this happens, except by the statement: "Behold, I am making all things new!" (Rev. 21:5). The Spirit makes new meaning about what otherwise wouldn't have meaning and doesn't without Its assistance. It puts flesh on what otherwise is the dry bones of things.

Yes, one has to be attentive to many things, but here I am being attentive to the living right before my eyes and to the life of things busy making themselves.

The Spirit accompanies these living things, each in its own "self" development, because It is self-emptying. Christians have spent centuries savoring the self-emptied character of the Son of God who "did not deem equality with God something to be grasped at" (Phil. 2:6). What I am savoring is the self-emptied character of the Spirit. What else would explain the individuation of every living thing becoming more and more itself, except a self-emptying ingredient in them that allows all of them to go about the work of doing their things, while being both the principal and the principle of their living. There is an astonishing reverence for each particular being in this self-emptying Spirit.

To narrow down the kenotic character of God to the Son is to think too narrowly since the Spirit is "of the same stock" as the Second Person of the Blessed Trinity who took "the form of a man." But the Third Person of the Blessed Trinity even more completely entered into and accompanies the particularity of every "man" and wren and tree and all of the rest of groaning things that have been seeking the completion of their natures "until now." Though unbeknown to them, this should not be unknown to the rest of us. We are right to imagine God's utter transcendence, but because it is God, it shouldn't be surprising that there is more to the story. We should let ourselves savor the remarkable immanence of the Spirit, which is the other half of the Jesus story.

The busyness of the birds reminded me of St. Paul's assertion that "all creation groans and is in agony even until now" (Rom. 8:22). Paul includes in his scope the species human, and its groaning. All groan as they "await the redemption of their bodies" (v. 23). Like the birds in the bush, humans have many different activities they are about. One of these perhaps is praying. Paul is unimpressed by the quality of his own praying and the praying others do. What he is impressed by is that "the Spirit makes intercession for us [the pray-ers] with groanings that cannot be expressed in speech"(v. 26). In short, there are three layers of groaners: all of creation, humans, and the Spirit who is counted among the rest of us as a groaner.

Paul connects the groaning that praying is, and the groaning of the Spirit accompanying it. And happily that "He who searches hearts knows what the Spirit means" (v. 27). Wouldn't it seem very small of God to create all of creation and take only a very minute portion of its groaning into account, that is, humans, and even more narrowly those who pray? In its own way a wren's chirping is its heart searching. Paul is sure that "God makes all things work together for good for those who love God and have been called according to his decree." (v. 28). Which decree? "Let there be light . . . sky . . . sea . . . night . . . day . . . living creatures . . . man" (Gen. 1:3–27). "God looked at everything he had made and found it very good" (v. 21). The decree of creation!

Creation was made not only to groan and expire. It was made to groan and be completed. The resurrection is where groanings are going. The resurrection of Jesus was "exhibit A" for the passing from groaning to joy. Only an anthropomorphic egocentric sectarian would be so niggardly as to think in smaller terms than "the decree" that had creation come to be in the first place. "Good" as it is, incomplete is also how it is now. My eye has been on the sparrow these last two days and I am seeing it in a new way.

April 5

I have been reading about the ability of the mouse to build its house and to do so with enough foresight to add an escape hole in its construction lest some danger appear at its entryway on the ground where it peeks out like a sentry examining what there is to see and how to meet its needs. (This information is in articles published in the journal *Nature*, January 17, 2013: Patrick Goymer, "Genes for Home Building," 312, and Hopi Hoekstra, "Discrete Genetic Modules Are Responsible for Complex Burrow Evolution.")

A molecular, evolutionary biologist from Harvard, Dr. Hopi Hoekstra, led a three-person team over a ten-year period of work in which they studied several species of mice, some called "deer" mice, others "oldfield" mice. Their interest was in trying to connect their burrowing habits with their DNA. Both species make tunnels for themselves, but the deer mouse makes a much smaller one without an escape route, whereas the oldfield mouse makes a much longer and deeper tunnel with an escape hole built into its construction.

When the scientists interbred these two mice species, they were interested in the relation between their genetic makeup and their related behavior. One thing they found was that the effect of the DNA was regional in the sense that three of the four regions of DNA in each interbred mouse played a part in determining how deep or shallow their burrowing went and whether an escape tunnel was part of it. But they also learned that their research still has a way to go to narrow the behavior down from these regions to a gene or genes. There is something more individuated that the DNA itself couldn't predict but that Hoekstra and team expect to predict once their information can get from these regions to particular genes.

The researchers believe that the value of their research is that it gives greater knowledge of the behavior of things in nature and will therefore provide greater knowledge about human nature. A deeper understanding of the genetic makeup of the mouse may help function to remedy genetic deficiencies in us.

Three thank-you's are appropriate here. One is to thank the Spirit of God in and for Itself and Its selflessness. Another is to thank the Spirit for prompting and assisting the scientists who are pursuing knowledge, notwithstanding whatever biases they might have in doing so. And, finally, to thank the researchers here for their perseverance, since we now know much more about these mice and, by extension, ourselves. We should also appreciate the reverence the Spirit has for letting things be themselves without cutting them loose as they "do their thing." The Spirit enfolds each of the *creata* uniquely and immanently. The Spirit is Lord of what lives but does so in a way that is uniquely self-emptied as we might be able to see here in the DNA of the mice.

April 7

We are always seeking new information to extend our knowledge beyond what we already know. We might even come to the realization that we are finite seekers looking for infinitude, a mortality hoping for an immortality, a physicality that won't end. With our degree of desire in mind, what is the scope of God's desires? Are they as wide as "the ends of the earth"? (Isa. 49:6). Do God's salvific intentions extend to all of creation?

According to the Suffering Servant prophecy, they do; they are not simply for the Servant and Israel; they are as wide as "the coastlands"! God directly invites the Servant to abandon his insularity. "It is too little for you to be my servant, to raise up the tribes of Jacob and restore the survivors of Israel; I will make you a light to the nations, that my salvation may reach to the ends of the earth" (vv. 5–6).

This Isaian text critiques not only a religious chauvinism or a tribalism, but implies a critique even of a human-centeredness that would view intra-human life as merely resources for us humans, or means to our ends, without having any worth in and of themselves.

This matter becomes more explicit as we awaken to the narrowness of our productivity, which hasn't taken into account the cost to the planet and its resources. The sustainability of the earth and its resources has not been in the picture; only our own sustainability has. Since green and grow have been presumed to go together, the consequence to the planet and its yellowing has been overlooked. Drought, global warming, the acidification of the oceans, overfishing, climate ruction, and so on are beginning to bring us out of our stupidity. An example of this naïveté: The oceans are 30 percent more acidic now than they were before the industrial revolution. Carbon emissions released into the atmosphere by humans are producing this acidification. Scientists predict that this assault on the well-being of the oceans will double by the end of this century. The oceans are a silent problem, but they are brimming with grave repercussions. Might it be however, is it even conceivable that the well-being of the coastlands and their oceans should become part of what God wants the religions to embrace in their respective ways of understanding what salvation is?

The first Servant Song, Isaiah 42:1ff., is even meatier or more tantalizing than the third one cited above, because it

gives more details about the awaited Servant and the scope of
his role and the expected manner of his accomplishment of it.
The Servant will be able to do what he has been called to do
because God says, "I have put my spirit upon him." The scope
of the Servant's role is nothing short of "bringing forth justice
to the nations." And nothing will stop him from performing
his task. "He will not grow faint or be crushed until he has
established justice in the earth" (v. 4). Oddly enough, he will
accomplish this task not by "lifting up his voice or by making it
heard in the street" but by being "as a covenant to the people,
a light to the nations" (v. 6). The text suggests that one part
of the Servant's task is to promote the recognition of the presence of "spirit" as already operating in people upon the earth
(v. 5). Nothing parochial about this spirit! The pneumatology
of Isaiah is universal. This alone should keep us from sectari-
anizing it, or imagining and believing that "some have it and
some don't," or narrowing the Spirit's range of interests to one
species rather than to all of life.

One of the sufferings the Servant is expected to undergo
is that he will be on the cusp between "new things" and "the
former things that have already come to pass" (vv. 8–9). One
thinks of the cry from the cross of Jesus: "Eloi, Eloi, lama sabac-
thani," as he personally laments the passing of the old creation
in his own dying, and bears witness to the new creation. It was
old not because the Spirit was absent from it but because Its
presence was not evident to those who had breath even as all
living things have had ever since there was breath.

According to Isaiah's pneumatology, the Holy Spirit of God
can be "grieved" (Isa. 63:10). How would one know it is? For
Isaiah, the heavens bear witness to this—in cries being emitted
from nature that is twisted. There are big steps moderns have
to take: (1) by personalizing the Spirit—as a person, it has a
will (1 Cor. 12:11); it can be grieved; (2) by reading the Spirit's
reaction to human behavior, including in seemingly impersonal

macro, hazardous weather conditions; (3) by moving from despair over our malfeasance as a species—all the way to hope, hoping against hope that "I am about to create new heavens and a new earth; the former things shall not be remembered or come to mind" (Isa. 65:17). The Isaian insight should help us to see that we are not aliens in nature and that eschatologically nature will cease to be inimical, for "the wolf and the lamb shall feed together, the lion shall eat straw like the ox; and there shall be no harm or ruin on all my holy mountain" (Isa. 65:25).

One way to know the will of the Person of the Spirit is through nature. If the Spirit is grieved by human behavior, conscience can register this. But the Spirit's grief can also be known in nature. The ten warmest years in the United States ever recorded were in the last fifteen years. Drought, hurricanes, and erratic weather patterns all generate the question: What is wrong, and are we humans a source of this turmoil? Increasingly the answer seems to be yes—we humans are the source of the turmoil that nature is manifesting. The heavens are telling not only the glory of God but also God's being upset about what we are doing to earth and who we think we are on it.

April 9

Belief is one thing; science is another; connecting them is a challenge. Here goes: Recently vents, hydrothermal vents, were discovered. They are found in rock formations deep within the earth. They spew forth water that can get as hot as 800 degrees Fahrenheit. These waters are loaded with chemicals and minerals. These spews result in a "riot of life" that is aswirl with thousands of species of things, some previously known (e.g., crab, barnacles, anemone, snails, starfish, shrimp); some heretofore unknown. They are all making a living for themselves in this milieu of this hot "chemical frenzy." (See "Hydrothermal Vents," a fourteen-page summary of the findings of the last forty years; and "Submarine Volcano" a similar résumé—both in Wikipedia.)

These hydrothermal vents were discovered for the first time in 1977 by surprised geologists near the Galapagos Islands in the Pacific Ocean. Since then similar vents have been found in a number of other sites, including in the Atlantic. Most recently one was found just a mile down in the ocean just north of Antarctica. A high-definition video camera placed 8,000 feet down in the dark waters sent back to the surface clear pictures of a whole world teeming with life from a site never seen before. Even more astonishing is that what has been found at one site is sometimes the same and yet often remarkably different from what is found in other sites. For example, at one site, worms as tall as a human but tubular and massive clams; at another, thousands of shrimp. What is even more surprising about this "sea vent life" is that whole life systems are being sustained by minerals and bacteria where there is no sunlight. The food chain is there, but light isn't. This fact alone confounds previous biological certainties.

How does something as similar as shrimp come from such diverse sites and even oceans apart? Part of the answer comes from geology and the also recent information that the earth's surface is composed of plates, twelve major ones. Each is moving slowly and not in the same direction. So, for example, when a plate moves apart or collides or slides past another plate, a crack can at times develop on the seafloor. Cold water flows into the crack and becomes superheated by the molten magma underneath, and the combination of these elements bursts up into the ocean and, voilà, a vent! A vent field creates a chimney-like plume that becomes a habitat for the ambient life-forms that hover around and feed off of it. All of this commotion seems to be why a particular species like shrimp can be found in vastly separated parts of the planet and nurtured by the distinctive food chain of particular vents. (Cf. Naomi Oreskes, *Plate Tectonics* [Westview Press, 2001]).

So while trying to make sense of these deep sea vents, each of which is spectacular in its own right, one also has to take into account the movement of plate tectonics. Knowledge of both of these is only now coming into the range of human awareness and putting the two together is helpful. It might help to imagine the whole earth as itself a kind of organism, something the Gaia hypothesis of James Lovelock proposed some decades ago. I'm trying to digest these large lumps of information. Everything seems to depend on or be connected to everything else. So: the eruption of a hydrothermal vent is contingent on a movement of the earth's crusts. And while I'm marveling at all of this, I also want to add this factoid: "compared to the surrounding sea floor, the hydrothermal vent zones have a density of organisms 10,000 to 1,000,000 times greater" than their nearby, relatively cool, calm zones. How odd of God to create in all these ways!

All of this has been going on for millions of years, and we never knew it. Today's vent can close and another open tomorrow. What meaning does the hydrothermal vent and all the life that surrounds it have, besides the physical, empirical data that is at the core of many sciences such as marine biology, geology, chemistry, biochemistry, genetics, seismology, nutrition, physics? Each of these distinct bodies of knowledge becomes more understandable the more interdisciplinary it becomes.

But, is there a *transdisciplinary* source of meaning to all of this kind of information? There is the challenge to make into a whole the knowledge that comes in bits from such different sources. One source of such a whole is the organizing story of faith in Christ. Like their ancestors, Christians try to fit new discoveries into the parameters of their faith story so as to make a whole of fact, faith, and reason. If they can do that, they might begin to learn how the son, the "first born of all creatures" has been the source of all the processes by which "everything on earth was created" and is why "everything continues in being" (Col. 1:17).

This is a lot to take in at one time.

April 10

Add to the aforesaid: there are a number of mountain ranges—all under water—which seem to circle the globe. It is from this chain that these volcanic-like vents erupt. So we can conclude that all of this shows providence at work and shows how *God makes stuff that makes itself* with each piece having a part to play in the well-being of the next. Although that is a comforting and faith-filled conclusion to come to, there's also the bad news. Like what? Like tsunamis (Japanese for "harbor wave") that kill many people and can unsettle whole nations! These irregularities come from the same kind of plate movements that generate hydrothermal vents. Yet without these kinds of unpredictable eruptions many of the organisms on planet earth would never have lived or would not continue to live. Neither would we, therefore.

If we had only the high Christology as we have mentioned here in the letter of the Colossians, we would have to wonder about how to connect that Letter's Christ figure to this hypothermal vent data in a way that could explain them in a unitary narrative. It seems that without the Person of the Spirit as the Lord and Completer of such things as hydrothermal vents and plate tectonics that belief in the personhood of Christ could stretch into unintelligibility. It is much easier to believe that through him *and* the Spirit "everything on earth was developed" and that *through and in Them* "everything continues in being." When the letter to the Colossians was being written,

pneumatology as an essential ingredient of the developing faith
metanarrative was still in its infancy. The mystery of the Trinity
was still emerging in the minds and hearts of Jesus' followers
rather than a fully emergent doctrine.

One of the beautiful products or results of the presence of
the Spirit in the world is solidarities, even ironic solidarities:
wholes that allow the parts to stay themselves and continue
doing their seemingly separate thing. Hence the connection
between the ruction of the plates and hydrothermal vents and
anorganic and organic life and the wherewithal for further
life to emerge—what's not to see in this remarkable interconnectedness! And, of course, while the thrall of solidarity can
be savored, one still has to take in the irony of death emerging
from the very same phenomena producing life but now also
life from or through death. Both the solidarities and their
transmogrifications from death into life are part of the way
the Spirit led Jesus into his meaning and passion and death
and resurrection, and continues to do so for those who derive
their system of meanings from *Logos* and *Pneuma* under *Abba*.

The quintessential solidarity for the Christian metanarrative is the consubstantiality between the divinity and humanity
that was and is Jesus. This has been named in various ways
throughout the history of that faith, but two natures in one
person is the classical formula and it enjoys and still deserves
that understanding today.

This reflection represents an exercise in whole-making,
an effort produced through a natural methodology of being
"attentive, then intelligent, then reasonable and responsible."
That is Bernard Lonergan's methodology for describing the
steps that implicitly or explicitly go on in coming to making
wholes (see *Insight* [Longmans, Green, 1957]). Scientific data
needs further intelligibility to come to meaning. Theology tries
to connect faith within reason and what has been discovered
through reason with faith. The Spirit is Lord of the life of the

mind and the life of faith and the life of these millions of tiny organisms that flourish near these hypothermal vents. (See *PLoS Biology*, January 3, 2012, Public Library of Science—a peer-reviewed, open-access journal.)

April 12

Consciousness—what explains it? The sciences have suggested a number of directions in their attempt to explain it, and they continue to do so. The reigning twentieth-century theories have been first biological and then increasingly neurological. But the neurons in general and the brain in particular have so far been found insufficient in themselves for explaining consciousness. More recent theories have gone from biology to information, in particular to "information theory." The inquiry into how consciousness is explained by information deals with the question of whether the information in consciousness is observer-relative (its existence is generated by the observer) or independent of the informed observer (for example, the fact that George Washington was the first president of the United States informs the observer). This distinction is intriguing because obviously most or a lot of what informs us is observer-relative. This opens the field of consciousness for further questions about what explains it. I hope that pneumatology will eventually be helpful for explaining something about consciousness, whether observe-relative or observer-informed.

To be more explicit about this hypothesis of information theory for partially explaining consciousness, I will start by exploring it from three scriptural texts that were penned in different centuries by very different authors. Their observations, I believe, can be seen as pointing to the Spirit as a partial explanation about the consciousness operating in these different texts.

First, from Micah, who was a contemporary of the prophet Isaiah. He was quite upset about fraudulent merchants, corrupt priests, venal judges, and the exploitation of the poor going on in the land of Judah. He had been raised believing in the covenant God had made with his people. His sense was that God had had enough of all of these "ne'er do wells" and was going to bring a new ruler to Israel and Judah. He believed that this new ruler was going to have incredible power but was also going to be a shepherd not only for his people but for all peoples and would bring about peace to the ends of the earth. Micah believed this, hence the text! And Christians who have the same belief believe that Micah's prophecy (Mic. 5:1–4) came true with the coming of Jesus and that he was the proof of its truth. Belief believes that something is observer-independent. Nonbelief would make this observer-dependent.

The second text is a Psalm, which of course is a prayer being prayed/written to God by the Psalmist. It becomes observer-independent to a believer who can appropriate it with the help of the Spirit and the believing community. "O Shepherd of Israel, hearken from your throne upon the cherubim, shine forth. Rouse your power and come to save us . . . this vine that your right hand has planted! " (Ps. 80). The Psalmist's belief is observer-independent, even though the hoped-for Shepherd hasn't come yet.

The third text is from the Gospel of Luke (1:39–45). Mary was in need of a confirmation that she had heard something about reality. She received this confirmation from the greeting Elizabeth gave her! "Filled with the Holy Spirit," Elizabeth cried out in a loud voice: "Blessed are you among women and blessed is the fruit of your womb. . . . Blessed are you who believed that what was spoken to you by the Lord would be fulfilled." Elizabeth's consciousness confirmed Mary's. Both believed they themselves were not the authors of what was in their consciousness, and there was the evidence of this in each of their wombs. What was happening to both of them was not only in their wombs but that God who was independent of them had chosen to be dependent on them and had inspired their consciousness (as well as Zechariah's and Joseph's) to consent to what all of them were experiencing. In short, the Spirit assisted their consciousnesses and freed them from other winds that would have blown their discernments about reality off course.

Though these three texts had multiple authors, all three have one author in common. That author was the Spirit. It might be the further explanation that science is still looking for to explain consciousness. If the Spirit is "the Lord and Giver of Life," the life of the brain and the mind, might it also be of consciousness? If one is operationally vectored to know reality, it seems its mission is the same as the Spirit's. Its mission is to lead *all* into *all* truth.

The fact that so much that goes on in our consciousness doesn't rise to anything necessarily consequential or religious or to things that are observer independent does not prove or disprove that consciousness is Spirit accompanied. Even though consciousness and Spirit are not separated even when the contents of consciousness are trivial, the famous Lonergan adage applies here: "Objectivity is the fruit of authentic subjectivity." The Spirit's agenda in human consciousness is to assist it in its effort to grasp and to be grasped by objective reality.

Again I marvel at the Spirit's self-emptied selflessness that has been going on since the beginning of life. It is about time to end this anonymity. Consciousness and the Spirit will be intertwined forever, Amen! Whether the attained knowledge is observer-independent or observer-dependent, the Spirit's assist accompanies it.

Of course, observer-dependent knowledge can be true or false. For example, when Elizabeth exclaimed that Mary was blessed among all women and that the fruit of her womb was blessed and that the mother of her Lord came to her in the person of Mary—her knowledge was true. As was Luke's information that was included in this scenario in his Gospel. "Observer-dependent" can mean one of two things. It can mean that what the observer says names reality. The Magnificat of Mary did. Or it can mean it only has the fragile ontological status of what one mind gives it. Then the claimed knowledge could be false, and to that extent belongs in the category of misunderstanding or misinformation, maybe even a lie. It has no future beyond what the deceived observer gave it.

In brief, where are we with this purported insight into consciousness? I'm not sure it helps to explain the phenomenon of consciousness. It doesn't help to differentiate believers from nonbelievers. A nonbeliever can be bereft for a whole lifetime of the deeper insights and meanings that some consciousnesses come to live from and on. <u>The reductionist empiricist has an</u> *Tina?* <u>a priori conviction that faith-knowledge isn't about anything real, whereas the believer finds life's deepest meaning in it.</u>

The part of the Good News that is poorly and seldom told is that God has entrusted humans with a consciousness so that humanity can come to knowledge assisted by the Spirit of God. If the knowledge is authentic, it is kingdom building. If it is not accepted as true, it could mean that it is only a matter of time till it is, because of the limitations of this present moment of knowledge, which presumably will be superseded by further knowledge (including about consciousness).

April 14

Much has been learned from neuroscience about consciousness; nonetheless consciousness keeps eluding full understanding. Neuron firings and all the other complexities uncovered by science, such as neurotransmitters, are not enough to explain it. The subjectivity of consciousness is elusive.

I want to go back to the new development in the quest to know what consciousness is, namely information theory (Christof Koch, *Consciousness: Confessions of a Romantic*

Reductionist [MIT Press, 2012]). Information incites consciousness. An alive consciousness is one that has some information.
This idea, however, produces a problem: What about machines
such as smart phones or personal computers that contain much
information? Are they to be considered in the same family
as consciousness? Koch, obviously, distinguishes biological
consciousness from the rest of information carriers.

Koch also sees that there is something fundamentally
different from the material brain causing experience and the
experience of what one is conscious of that is not reducible
to its physicality or biology. So, he posits that "consciousness
is a fundamental, an elementary, property of living matter."

Again, my interest is in the contents of the information
and whether these contents are observer-dependent (produced
by the person or persons) or observer-independent (information out there, which is appropriated by the consciousness).
To go back to the assertions made by Elizabeth about Mary
who had just come to visit her. Where did she get the information she had, according to the Gospel of Luke, about Mary?
"Blessed are you among women . . . (you who are) the mother
of my Lord" (Luke 1:41). According to the text, she had such
information because "she was filled with the Holy Spirit" (v.
40). So she was dependent, in this case, on what she learned
because the Holy Spirit somehow informed her about her
cousin from Nazareth. It was too far from the "hill country
of Judah" for her to have had any other way of knowing
about Mary's annunciation experience. It was very important
information for Mary, who would have had to wonder about
the stature of the infant in her womb. Elizabeth confirmed
Mary's consciousness about what she was being asked to be
and do and produce and become.

I go back to my assertion that the Spirit accompanies consciousness and has been doing so ever since there was such a phenomenon
in humans. Although it is rare in Scripture for the product of a

human consciousness to be directly ascribed to the Holy Spirit, that infrequency is not fatal for pressing the question.

There is an obvious difference between consciousness that is always information seeking and conscious truth-finding or reaching satisfactory conclusions. What is not as obvious is whether there is any connection between the everyday truth we have to weigh and what Jesus promised to send in the Person of the Spirit (John 16:13). The promise is that "he will guide you to all truth."

What was the connection between this "Spirit of truth" that Jesus promised his hearers and the true judgments, accurate conclusions they and everyone else contemporary with them had been coming to, as well as all those in all the eras and ages and moments before Jesus named this Spirit and all true judgments made since then? Could it be that the Spirit of truth has been accompanying human consciousness all along? It is a question eminently worth asking, pursuing, testing. I will argue for an affirmative answer. Notice, accompanying not intervening. Not vertical interventionism but horizontal assistance. Most information is socially transmitted. Some of it not of great worth; some of it essential. Like—Is the shadow before my car in the night a person in which case I have to slam on the brakes or just something originating from my imagination? Is my intuition about a person something I should take seriously or just a fleeting, dismissible impression? Judging information and the issue of the Spirit's assistance is what I am wondering about specifically. The more religious the contents, the easier the connection can be made. It is harder to make the claim the more "secular" or everyday-ish the information coming into my consciousness is.

But wouldn't it seem terribly small of Jesus and in turn of God to give the ability to come to knowledge of the truth only to those who followed his Son? No one before Jesus had ever put together Spirit and truth and named it the Spirit of truth. Though this idea was first heard in the Qumran community, it wasn't imagined to be referring to a person. True, there were prophets and seers and kings who had the Spirit ascribed to them in discrete bursts. But the Last Supper discourse in John is, among other things, a naming ceremony for the distinct personhood of the Spirit and I believe its role in civilization of coming to know what is true observer-independent.

Why would it not be right to be grateful and give glory to the Spirit for all the things that were to be learned subsequent to Jesus' announcement about the Spirit? And also to be grateful to the Spirit for all the things that were learned before Its distinct personhood was disclosed? And for all knowledge therefore? And while we're at it, to also give glory to Jesus since in the same passage, he claims that "all that the Father has belongs to me." So here we have an implicit Trinitarian ascription about the matter of consciousness and information.

My point simply is that for a fuller explanation of consciousness, we need to attend to the pneumatological dimension of it. And as to the information that is the contents of consciousness—very little of it is explicitly about God. Nonetheless, it could be that Spirit has been accompanying it all the centuries before Jesus and his Last Supper discourse to make the connection. If this is so, that would bespeak a very patient God and a very selfless Spirit who has been assisting so many for so long with no acknowledgment. If coming to truth is what is being assisted and being brought to birth all the years of human existence, our praise of the Spirit of truth is long overdue.

I am not blaming the Spirit for the errors and misuses of consciousness that all have been guilty of. Nor do I want to put a quantitative proportion of its misuse and its good use. What might add some credibility to this linking of truth-seeking and truth-finding and truth-telling and the Spirit of truth is that no one ever desires the untrue. No matter how bent out of shape we might be, we want to know the facts, the truth, and the real so we can put this information to work. We want to know if we are wrong or being deceived or uninformed about something. One part of consciousness that is usually more alert to truth than the rest of it is conscience. But even conscience can be dulled by not wanting to listen to the truth.

Unless and until experts about consciousness come up with a better explanation, I will take the theology of knowledge that Jesus supplies in these few lines in John as being as good as it is going to get. "Consecrate them in the truth. . . . I consecrate myself for them so that they may also be consecrated in truth" (John 17:17–19). And if this assistance has been operating in us and in all people all along, petition for it would seem appropriate.

It seems to me that confining the work of the Spirit to inspiration and revelation and matters religious has done a grave injustice to the omnipresence of the Spirit in human consciousness. There is the need to connect consciousness and Spirit to the vast, countless oceans of divine activity that are not and therefore should not be limited by us to religious moments.

Implicit in the above is that the Spirit has been a source of knowledge not only about God but also about knowledge of all reality itself. There has been a dependency on Spirit ever since consciousness became operational. If it is true that knowledge and knowledge of the Spirit should be linked one to another, as well as coming to knowledge of what is not so and not true, the praise of God, in particular, the Spirit of Truth is long overdue!

April 15

Although the scriptures are believed by believers to be inspired, they also have been seen as having human authors. If these scriptural authors had the knowledge of nature that was contemporary with their eras, what was the knowledge of *physics* that John had, for example, when he wrote the Gospel? And what difference would our knowing this make? The skeptic would ask: Since we in the twenty-first century are so much more knowledgeable about physics than John was, how can his meager or even mistaken understanding of nature make what he wrote believable? Simple believers would respond that his was an inspired, religious knowledge, so what difference does it make that he was ignorant about physics? So maybe there is a third possibility. A recent work by Gitte Buch-Hansen, *It Is the Spirit That Gives Life* (Copenhagen: Gruyter Press, 2010) represents knowledge of the metaphysics of Stoicism that was contemporary with John. (Stoicism dated from the third century BCE to the middle of the sixth century CE.) Buch-Hansen's thesis is that the Johannine Spirit can be better understood if one sees the context of John's understanding of pneumatology in light of Stoicism.

Stoicism saw nature as one, as a whole, and as good. It saw humans' ethical responsibility as having to live in accordance with this Whole (65). It saw abetting nature as the way to be moral; diminishing it as immoral. The whole of nature was organic, one whole composed of bodies in movement vis-à-vis one another. Nature had two principles that can be abstracted from the movements of bodies in motion. There is a passive principle and an active one. The passive principle is matter that is "substance without quality," and the active principle has God as "the Artificer of each thing throughout the whole extent of matter." This is according to Diogenes Laertius who wrote the classical work on the nature of Stoicism for his day (66). His Stoic belief was that "God is one and the same with Reason, Fate and Zeus. . . . In the beginning he was by himself. . . . He created first all the four elements, fire, water, air, earth; these together constitute unqualified substance or matter" (67).

So this father of Stoicism thought that all these phenomena that are perceived as differentiated from one another nevertheless are "all as parts of the Whole, in touch with one another." Stoicism further believed that a universal *pneuma* was the source of the whole and of all these differentiations. It also believed that pneuma "is simultaneously the source of cohesion and the stability of the differentiated parts, and of the unity, coherence and interrelatedness of the Whole. . . . There is no event, however small, that does not affect the Whole" (78). Nor is there any event that is beyond pneuma's reach.

The Danish author Buch-Hansen sees Stoic pneuma as the inspiration for the pneumatology of John. Its immaterial materiality is what makes divine and human and material interconnectedness comprehensible. If no pneuma, no meaning; but with pneuma, the meaning of God, nature, and worship all emerge and converge. Her way of seeing John's Gospel through the lens of the physics of Stoicism is very interesting, but not finally convincing, since even with Stoicism, knowledge will emerge gradually and will not be sent from above.

If John's pneumatology were foundationally Stoic, the events in his Gospel would be seen in a different light, especially spatially. For example, the ascension would presume the truth of a three-tiered cosmology. A Stoic reading of John's Gospel could help free us from the three-tiered cosmology of up there and down there and here. But Buch-Hansen's thesis has not been convincing to Johannine scholars who know a lot more about that Gospel and Stoicism than I do, so I will accept their better judgment (e.g., Cornelia Bennema's book review in *Review of Biblical Literature*, 2011, by the Society of Biblical Literature).

April 16

This morning I "did" a baptism. The reading for the service was: "Flesh begets flesh; Spirit begets Spirit" (John 3:6). These six words of Jesus to Nicodemus seem to me to be the clearest words in all of Scripture for either the linking or the delinking of the empirical and the theological. But there are three other words that Jesus didn't say but would have, I think, if asked. I will say them because they sum up what I want to convey in this book: Spirit begets flesh! This is a riff on believing there is nothing that has been made that God is not the Creator of. And on believing that through the Logos all things were made. Or on believing that there is nothing living that does not come from the Lord and Giver of Life who is the Spirit. The flesh that believes these Trinitarian truths about its life can be carriers and mediators of the Spirit.

There is no antithesis between flesh and spirit. Flesh *is* because Spirit *is* and because Spirit is "the Giver of Life." Flesh is beholden to Spirit for its life. Absent that knowledge, flesh is ignorant about itself. Ignorant flesh begets more of same, flesh alive but ignorant of the whence and why and whither of its life. As if that's not enough, ignorant flesh begets ersatz spirit like ideologies, rationalizations, and secularized ways of living, as well as any number of forms of distraction from the Spirit as to its whence and why and whither. Flesh is instrumental in begetting life, but it cannot beget spirit.

The belief behind every sacrament is that God can bring Spirit to flesh. Different things function as the empirical-here-and-now medium that is used to have this come about—like bread, wine, oil, water, and the sacramentality of nature. Take baptism, for example, and water. The water of baptism doesn't bring the baptized into the community of faith; the living faith of the Spirit-bearing community does. Spirit begets Spirit. And

Paul?!

the community of faith commits itself to socialize the baptized into the saving story that has become a Spirit-bearing community. The water plus the faith of the baptizers plus the Spirit—these three seal the deal, presuming the baptized buys the package of being named in the Father, the Son, and the Holy Spirit. So, Spirit-bearing flesh can beget "spirit."

What can diminish this passage of flesh to spirit with the sacraments is formalism, going through the motions or becoming observers of their being confected. For example, Eucharist . . . attending as if <u>a spectator detached</u> from the community and exiting the premises, a wafer-ed solipsist. <u>What diminishes the passage of flesh to spirit in nature is an eye that is skeptical or a mind that doesn't transcend naturalism.</u>

April 17

On the seafloor of the Pacific Ocean there are organisms, bacteria, to be precise, that are living, and have been alive for more than a thousand years . . . and for all we know now, they could have been living for millions of years.

This information makes me want to connect these things: the Christian Creed's belief that the Spirit is the Lord and Giver of Life and all of this knowledge we now have about living bacteria, and both of these in light of Bernard Lonergan's theory of emergent probability. As conscious and believing human beings, we can pick up from these newly discovered deep ocean entities and connect them to their Lord who is the source of their living and moving (though not too far) and having their being. There are many millions, trillions of these bacteria down there. <u>They are incalculably old but still living</u>—86 million years old according to one study by Leon Watson in *Science* (May 22, 2012).

If the sovereignty of the Spirit goes as deep as the ocean floor and has done so for that long, where doesn't it? While savoring such information, we can extend our praise of God back to before the emergence of *Homo sapiens* and all the way back to when these many creatures emerged.

We know enough biology, and here microbiology, to be able to differentiate living things from nonliving things. Living things have a metabolism. They are autopoietic, that is, self-organizing. On what does the metabolism of these ageless bacteria live? On other living organisms, themselves autopoietic, and on chemical compounds minute enough to be appropriated by the bacteria. These are sources of energy for bacteria's purposes, the main one of which obviously is to continue to be. Another of these is reproduction, whatever that is in their case. Another of these is to compound *inter se*; bacteria are mutualizers. They live on oxygen, however, puzzling that is, since they are buried in the sediment of the ocean. Finally water—like all that lives, they need water. It is plentiful in the Atlantic as well as the Pacific. Water is something oceans have plenty of.

This knowledge of ocean floor study of bacteria keeps us from looking at life within our own time scale. These bacteria are the original ancients. It follows that since the watch on the wrist of the Spirit doesn't calculate things in terms of seconds, minutes, hours, days, years, centuries, millennia, etc., then neither should we.

Without bacteria there would be no biomass in the world, and therefore, no us. While the questions that are answered by microbiology are many, the questions which emerge from even a smattering of the microbiological knowledge becoming available to us multiply instead of diminishing. The more we know about bacteria, the more we know about ourselves.

Since a bacterium can live 86 million years, what does it do all the day long? All millennia long? Whether one or many, I believe they praise God in their own bacterial way. So, given this scenario, what at present and in the long run would be a worthwhile activity for humans to undertake before undertakers do their thing with each of us? We too could praise God, an action we could grow in to accompany our growing in knowledge of nature. The ways of God and nature and human nature all coincide. Bacteria are not going to be bored to death, nor are they going to die, so we might learn something from them.

One way humans praise God even inadvertently is by making wholes—connecting this to that. Praise can be slipshod if we are content to stay ignorant when there is knowledge available about things. Evan Thompson's *Mind in Life* (Belknap Press of Harvard University Press, 2007) is a good example of the attempt at whole-making. His subtitle indicates the three lumps of the whole he is seeking to put together: "Biology, Phenomenology, and the Sciences of Mind."

One of Thompson's insights is that biological life is not only self-organizing but also in very differing degrees, cognitional. A bacterium has a mind of its own, so to speak. This needs to be taken into account if we want to see how in humans the bodily connects to the cognitional. And if bacteria are quasi-cognitional, imagine what the neuron is! Our mental life is voracious because of neurons. Thompson seeks to narrow the gap between consciousness and nature without being reductionist.

The self-organization of a bacterium and a neuron, and the self-organization of a thought . . . can these be correlated? His 500-page book gives an understandable account of the workings of "mind in life." The route Thompson goes to explain that the way material substrates and consciousness work together is through phenomenology, Husserl's "transcendence-within-immanence," to be precise. The subdiscipline that has emerged from this direction is a neurophenomenology that is a quasi-scientific philosophical effort to explain the nexus between subjectivity and objectivity. I miss the insight pneumatology could bring to his impressive work. It doesn't "work" otherwise, it seems to me. The distinct teleologies of so many "parts" of us pull into a convergence that my will alone doesn't satisfactorily explain.

April 19

My interest in the brain and some of the new things neuroscience has been learning about is increasing daily. What is my own mind's relation to this neural activity of my brain? How does my mind depend on my brain and yet transcend it? The best prescientific human minds have for centuries been trying to understand our minds via the transcendental notions of the true, the good, the beautiful, or being, and so on. Here I will be more empirical.

Being ignorant of science is not a good way to do theology. (Of course, as already noted, the sciences should not be content to be ignorant of theology either.) As science is learning more and more about the brain, I will try to add what little we know about the Spirit to this new knowledge of the brain. But it is only a sliver. As Jesus said: our knowledge of the Spirit is a little like our knowledge of the wind—almost nothing about where it comes from or where it is going and therefore taking us. The mind is the interlocutor between the brain and the Spirit. Before we can figure out how these three might be understood together or more as a whole I want to have a look at each of them separately.

We humans haven't known very much about the human brain until fairly recently. Nineteenth-century phrenology was the first inept effort at this. But the more we learn about the brain now, the more astonishing it is. It didn't evolve into its present "homo sapiential" condition of development until about 40,000 years ago. On an evolutionary timeline this makes the human brain a very recent entry in the already existing world of nature. A future wonder: for those who don't get dizzy counting, in the ordinary brain there are a <u>86 million neurons</u> or cells and even more support cells actively operating within its circuitry at any given period of time.

The brain is complex, so much more complex than even those who are considered the present experts in the field feel they have mastered. One of the sciences that has developed from our knowledge of the brain and its related questions is cognitive neuroscience. It is particularly interested in the neural substrates of mental processes and cognition. This discipline was not established as a sufficiently unified field of study until the 1970s. A number of scientific methods and subfields have grown from studies of cognitive neuroscience—like psychophysics, cognitive psychology, cognitive neuropsychology, cognitive psychophysiology.

What has been fascinating to those who know more and more about the brain is how all its myriad influences or varied <u>ingredients—neural, molecular, chemical, biological, electrical, genetic, hormonal</u>—keep seeking for new things, and for the most part succeed in putting together new things and old, you might say. Its incredible dynamisms, which are at base neural, synaptic firings, somehow work together to try to make wholes, especially when any number of sources of disequilibrium (physical, ideational, emotional, etc.) threaten to undo its usual equilibrium.

Before I learned any of these things about the brain I had conducted extensive interviews with faculty in a number of universities. I asked them to name for themselves and their colleagues "what 'the good' is that each of you is seeking to accomplish." I would sum up their answers—from more than two hundred persons I had gathered in a number of workshops at eight different universities between 2006 and 2008—as having this in common: they are seeking to make aggregates out of the disaggregated data they gather. Having now subsequently come to a bit of knowledge about neuroscience, I now find it interesting to see that the wholes these academics were pursuing in their respective fields were put together physiologically and *au naturel* by their brains, neurons, synapses, and so on. But Spirit is a Connector!

April 21

I have learned that there are more neurons presently operating in the brains of each one of us here on earth than there are stars in our galaxy. My response to that fact is awe! And that these neurons have been operating all my conscious life! Both gratitude and some degree of shame, that our brains, like our bodies and our lives, are so taken for granted!

But even more amazing is that these neurons are working all the time whether we are actively thinking or in a default mode, thinking about nothing, or even when we're sleeping—they are still working and organizing things for when we are conscious and consciously thinking. I am learning these things from the studies of Alvaro Pascual-Leone, whose work at Harvard Medical School is about the neural plasticity of the brain (see *The Paradoxical Brain* [Cambridge University Press, 2011]). His main interest is in finding out "the rules that are invariant across neural systems" so that he can produce a theory that gives "a coherent account of a neuro-cognitive theory."

He has also been interested in learning about the brain in its inactive states. It is not really at rest at those times as if it were awaiting a symphony to begin when our consciousness awakes—No, the brain at rest is already "the symphony consuming 20 times as much energy as the conscious life of the mind" according to Sharon Begley, another scientist. Pascual-Leone claims that "the bulk of the brain's activity" takes place when it is at rest and seemingly inactive. It seems that much of our brain activity as anticipatory; it is functioning in a prospective mode even when "our minds" are not working. Appreciation and gratitude extend downward to the most infinitesimal agencies operating without themselves sleeping while I am sleeping.

∞

April 22

Neurophysiological methods are finding out more about the connections between regional brain activation and the resulting human behavior. Much research has gone on in studies that seek to localize the particular site in the brain that seems to be the source of a given behavior, like the site from which speech emerges. Did you know that it is the parietal lobe of the left hemisphere of the brain? In general, it had always seemed like each one of our senses could only give us the data of one sense like touch or taste or smell or our visual or auditory capacities. But Pascual-Leone's experiments are finding that even when there are very specific sense deficiencies like blindness, the brain is able to act meta-modally, like it is able to be meta-regional and meta-sensory in the sense that it has distinct and efficient operators within it which make wholes by rewiring, even by extracting data derived from one sense and using it in another.

To put Pascual-Leone's hypothesis technically: "the development of functional specificity of cortical modules is the result of competition between expert networks that have distinct structural and functional properties (thus giving an indication of) a mechanism by which apparent crossmodal neuroplasticity occurs.... [Thus] cortical modules ... [which] should be thought of as being metamodal brain centers that perform particular computational operations without specific reference to a type of sensory input" (*Progress in Brain Research*, vol. 134 [2001]).

Science has contributed so much to our understanding of ourselves and continues to do so, and while its findings are necessary, the more science knows, it is often unable to answer some of the questions that surface. Just to stay with this particular subject matter: If the neurophysicality of the brain is a sufficient explanation of us and our choices, how would moral responsibility come about? We count among our most basic cultural assumptions that the good use of intelligence should be honored and its inept uses blamed; and freedom prized and criminality punished. None of these social constants would make any sense if there isn't more to us than the neurophysiological. Something transphysical, transneural, and trans-sensorial has to enter the picture somewhere to explain us to ourselves.

The question of where God is in these neural matters needs to be asked. Neuroscience provokes one to revisit his or her ideas about God. For example, when is the brain or its operations and physicality its own explanation and when is it not? Although one can be scientifically reductionist in trying to answer these questions, one can also be theologically reductionist and try to have everything explained by something supernatural and extrinsic to the brain.

One would have to be brain-dead to not experience one's brain as a living organ. The transcendent God is also radically immanent in all that is, in particular to all that is living and acting as the brain surely is. Likewise, imagining God, the Author of life, outside or up there or at a distance from the living brain, would be too mythic a way to imagine God or to think about what consciousness entails and needs. Another theological crudity that needs to be revisited is God as cause. Linear causality, the univocal way of imagining a cause preceding an effect or an effect following a cause, certainly does not exhaust the reality of causality. One way causality was handled in the past was by distinguishing a primary from a secondary cause. The distinction would have some value if it could account for how the cortical modules operating in the brain have God as their cause, and at the same time we are able to see them as their own causality.

All of which is to say that spatial and temporal images for seeing the activity of God in our lives are too simple to be satisfactory, because God is only analogously a cause. God is not an object among objects nor a cause among causes. To say that God is only analogously a cause means that God is somewhat like and somewhat unlike a cause in relation to our experience of causes. In fact, causing might be better cashiered as a verb in our cognitional processes to describe God's working in creation and replaced by the verb "participating." Every living thing is participating within the reality of the living God in its own particularity, individuality, and operationality. To arrive at this insight and belief in God as participating in minute waves, particles, neurons, and "metamodal brain centers" would take some doing. But it should be arrived at.

Yes, and the doing presumes praxis, the practice of worship. One can best experience through worship the kind of God who does not "interfere with or countermand the integrity and adequacy of the causal structures of nature or of history" (William Stoeger, SJ, "Conceiving Divine Action in a Dynamic Universe," in *Scientific Perspectives on Divine Action*, ed. Robert Russell, Nancey Murphy, and William Stoeger (University of Notre Dame Press, 2008), 231ff.). Thinking our way into a new way of seeing ourselves and God is not the only route we have. We can also act our way into a new way of thinking about God. This is the effect worship can have.

God doesn't affect mental life by commandeering people's minds but by assisting them and empowering them to see and take responsibility for their decisions and actions. If God wills to affect the world and, more specifically, humans, beginning in their consciousness and with their rationality and moral agency, and by extension through social, material, and moral progress, then it is evident that the body, more pointedly, the brain, seems to be where God prefers to effect this (Thomas Tracy, "Special Divine Action and the Laws of Nature," in Russell, Murphy, and Stoeger, 277ff.).

The ever-developing information we have about the architecture of the brain, therefore, and its overall operations, needs to be integrated with a willingness to revisit our understanding of both ourselves and God. Any ongoing correction of either or both of these has to go on if both reason and faith are to be integrated and if each is to have its own integrity. We have to keep trying to make a whole out of our developing experience and our growing understandings (here of the interactivity of the brain and God). Not trying to do so weakens and fragments identity. Insight into our own meaning and God's is never a cheap trip, nor is it attained once and for all.

May 1

In light of all this cognitive neuroscientific information, a unitary case for mind has to be made, hence for subjectivity and consciousness, and therefore for questions, insight, judgment, doubt, error. The whole history of philosophy and its corollary, epistemology, has been dealing with these categories. I might add, much of the careers of the two most famous phenomenologists, Edmund Husserl and Maurice Merleau-Ponty, was spent composing an argument against psychoneural reductionism. They had a special appreciation for the transcendental capacity of the mind vis-à-vis objects perceived within *consciousness*. They were trying to figure out how the brain works, knowing full well that mind is its own emergent, though beholden to brain matter. Yes, but brain matter *sans* mind would be useless just as mind without brain would have to be angelic or an imaginary.

Our intending is continually moving. The dynamisms that move us are notions. They seek a content, and often move to concepts. The notions move the neural activity within our brains in the direction of a specific something that is true, or good, or beautiful. As this present material suggests, the brain even when it is seemingly at rest is actually prospecting in the direction of these three transcendental notions. So the neurons collectively are foraging not in general but always into the particulars of one of the triangularities, the true, the good, and the beautiful. It seems to me that that the classical transcendental notions at work in human intentionality could be seen as the Spirit at work, beginning with the initial neural, physiological level of our cognition. There is, in other words, a pneumatology at work in cognition in both its notional and its most material starting points.

Something has to account for how the physiology of this three-pound structure, which we call a brain, produces the extraordinary things that it produces! If it is not the brain, is it the mind that explains humans' ability to know and act on their knowledge, and to choose and do the good, to affect nature and decrease chance and to build edifices and generate cultures, etc.? How is it that these two levels of capacity, the physical and the mental, are able to do one thing? Where does this capacity for whole-making come from? How do we get from a complex congeries of genes, neurons, synaptic firings, etc., to explain the simple act of cognition?

My suspicion is that the more we know about physiology the more we will know about—physiology. And even as we learn more about how thinking emerges from matter scientifically, the obscurity will continue. Science alone will leave one meaning-starved. The suggestion here is that the sooner we connect the brain cells or neurons and the notions with the Spirit, the more meaning we can arrive at about all three.

One's brain is not a sufficient explanation of the things that go on in it. Like wonder! How does all of this physical material emerge and become mind, and result in conclusions or questions or actions or wonder? Simply, whence questions? History is question-and-answer laden. The next move is to seek understanding from those who have had similar questions and have arrived at answers that satisfied them then.

May 2

So, to put all the preceding about consciousness together in terms of horizons: The first is the presence of physical objects themselves. The second is about what consciousness of the material in the first horizon wonders about and asks questions about. The third horizon comprises the cultures and the many conclusions one can learn through those "who've been there" and who have yielded up answers to their questions. We know that many of the rich ideas have come from prescientific culture. Anyway, there is energy in all three of these horizons. All three of these horizons are necessary to come to knowledge and meaning. It's not the brain that inquires or has questions; questions start off in horizon number 2, which I would call, generically, the mind. Nevertheless, I can't pursue my questions without being rooted in horizon number 1 and having some access to horizon number 3. So we are all in this together till death do us part.

Learning about cognitive neuroscience recalls to my mind again one of my favorite authors, Bernard Lonergan, and how he explained the different operations of our consciousness. In his writings he alluded to neural patterns, processes, and demand functions, but at the time of his writing (the 1940s through the '70s) not much was known about them. Now that we know much more about them, I recall his first transcendental precept: "be attentive." So now I am more specifically attentive to what we have been using all our lives probably without ever adverting to it, namely our neurophysiologically active brains.

Every brain has its own inner workings—even the brain of the worm. Its workings go from where it is to where it gets to next. Let's call this its teleology or to put it anthropologically, its purpose. Horizon-culture number 3 indulges in the category of finality here. Finality might not be the best term if it seems to imply a static worldview rather than an emergent, evolutionary teleology. Anyway, that caution having been lodged, let me continue with the language of finality because I take finalities not as ends in themselves but as orientations to ends.

Lonergan distinguishes three such orientations, horizontal, vertical, and absolute. Within every observable entity there is a finality in the sense that each is trying to get somewhere beyond where it is. If it is a vegetable, it may only be to get to water or whatever nutrients make it grow to continue its life cycle. If it is an animal, it may seek the same but will also seek to reproduce itself without having to have a sense of identity to reproduce. Horizontal finality has the horizon of its own good as its end.

Vertical finality is less evident in the rest of nature and more evident in humans. Humans' propensity is to pursue purposes that are for their own well-being like the rest of nature, but they can also pursue an end higher than their own good. Each cell, each neuron, each entity including humans is autopoietic in the sense of having its own horizontal teleology. But vertical finality enters the picture through the self-assembling interiority of the human person, who by nature or grace dreams up or is socialized into longer, deeper purposes and pursues them. Vertical finality presumes some orientation and capacity to desire and pursue ends higher than simply what is proportionate to a good within its own horizon of being. It is able to be self-emptied enough to act in light of the perceived higher good, hence vertical and operating in a vertical finality.

The finality of a given cell, a brain cell, for instance, operates within a very constricted horizon; an organism operates

within a larger horizon. Some finality is written into living things
in their most discrete parts and into the whole that makes it
an organism. But it is difficult to understand how horizontal
finality can get to vertical finality and vectored in the direction
of the giving of the self over to a higher end than to its own
good. The cause of vertical finality may be only circumstantial
or unanticipated. I think of the vertical finality entailed in the
care of a spouse who becomes disabled or develops dementia.

Lonergan completes this ladder of finalities with an absolute
one. Absolute finality describes being able to go for broke in the
desire for God and God's ways and for taking the means with
which one has been equipped to aspire to this, the apogee of
finality. The issue here is the desire for something beyond the
limitations that other horizontally and vertically vectored entities are confined to. This desired absolute may be for someone
or for a union or participation with something. For most of
the history of *Homo sapiens,* the species, this "something"
has been "God" in any number of the ways its members have
construed this absolute.

There doesn't seem to be a need to argue to the fact of
the first three kinds of finalities or to elaborate further on the
differences, since most of us presumably have an experience of
them. What is not self-evident is why there are such orientations
as well as the restlessness that seems to be scripted into all the
creata. And this absolute finality is also sufficiently known by
us. It is absolute in the sense that it transcends the conditions
that everything else seems to be limited by. It promises a *more*
than the other finalities.

The logic of the category of absolute finality is that if there
is any meaning or value in vertical finalities, they in turn have
to go somewhere. This somewhere is to a vertex of complete
meaning. (A vertex is the highest point of a triangle, the furthest
away from the base.) Reflection on personal experience is that
my activities, though always particular, are seldom ad hoc or

piecemeal. I have finalities in view or in mind. Human activities are ordinarily gathered toward wholes beyond a discrete act here or there. We are always leaving where we are and trying to get to something more. So, finalities are not abstractions. They are intrinsic to human intentionality. They describe patterns of desires and actions taken on them. We can see patterns of desire within all the created. Hence all of nature is scripted with finalities. All of which is one long gloss on the insight that has been at the headwaters of this volume, namely the Spirit as the Connector that generates finalities!

May 4

I am not intending here an apologia for transcendence. Rather I am intending an explanation of how one can put together the odd human combination of being part of earth while seeking for more. Lonergan is again helpful in naming meaning in its several realms. There is commonsense meaning, which is self-explanatory; there is theory meaning, which is equally self-explanatory. Less clear is a third realm, transcendent meaning. Like absolute finality, there is something breathless about this classification until one reflects on one's experience about the unknown that one has a sense of but can never get enough of. In most cases that unknown would be God, though the conception of what this unknown is, to say the least, is all over the place. All three of these experienced sources of meaning, that is, common sense, theory, and transcendence, are accessible without one's having to be a philosopher or a theologian or a psychologist or a mental gymnast. Though these descriptive terms are abstract, they convey the concrete experiences of the self we all have and have had.

The least accessible of all of the realms of meaning is a fourth one, which Lonergan calls interiority. It is the least accessible because it is closest to the bone of who we are. There is a self that undergirds all one's conscious acts. Interiority seeks knowledge of what is going on in the self and the value of it, as well as one's intentions or purposes or goals. Being conscious of one's own subjectivity in light of what one seeks and their value unearths this foundational meaning generator, which is interiority. One doesn't have to be a Lonerganean to see that these several classifications—the notions, finalities, and realms of meaning—are helpful in introducing one to oneself. At least they have been for the writer.

An overview of these last entries requires a final note. Since our experiences of ourselves and others are not easily named, they need to be understood as if we could stand outside of ourselves. This is what I find with Lonergan's understanding of the self. He names what we experience but seldom name. For example, he names interiority as the place where meanings are born. The transcendental notions is another Lonergan contribution. He wasn't the first to construe these, but he is the first one, at least in my readings, who could distinguish their relationship to the immediacies and particularities we live in and with. And finalities, too; we don't usually stand back from them to see that we are always heading to a "magis," to a more of some kind. Any or all of his categories give us a better way to name what goes on in us; at least I have found them to be so.

May 5

I would like to submit a further word, a theological one, on the above troika of brain, mind, and Spirit. As a species, *Homo sapiens* has been acting beyond its limits through praxis since time immemorial. We humans have been putting wholes together out of parts. The two parts: our physicality and embeddedness in nature and our transcendentality and multiple ways of making meaning.

Worship has been bringing the brain, mind, and Spirit into an alignment ever since *Homo sapiens* emerged on earth. According to the most recent studies in neuroscience, practices of worship have consequences on the neurons, and mind, and bodily health, and vice versa. These practices can be solitary, like yoga, or communal, like a Mass. They can be slow, like centered prayer, or fast, like the whirling dervish's dance. They can be formulaic or self-generated. They can be Catholic, Protestant, Jewish, Hindu, Moslem, etc. As practices, they necessarily involve the body, habit, and memory. Worship necessarily involves the neurons of the brain and affects the mind and all the relationships.

The neurons of the brain and religious practices and the workings of the Spirit in the operations of consciousness are all intertwined. The distances we tend to import into the differentiations between the spiritual and the physical, the mind and the body, the mental and the neural, the religious and the natural, the secular and the mystical—these are more a tribute to our ignorance than neuroscience would admit or say.

Neuroscientists Anne Benvenuti and Elizabeth Davenport elaborate on the effect religious practices have on the conscious mind. One of these is that there is a sense of belonging to a larger whole than the self has without such practices. They supply the evidence for these practices having neural effects on the brain and vice versa. They are not shy about suggesting that theologians need to learn this kind of information to show the compatibility between body and religion. "The inner workings of religious experience can now be measured in and described by the neural processes of the brain" ("The New Archaic," in A *Field Guide to a New Meta-field*, ed. Barbara Stafford [Chicago: University of Chicago Press, 2011], 31). They show how religious praxis affects the neuroarchitecture of the brain and situates the knower within "the greater whole of reality" or "within the nest of holarchies within which the knower exists and upon which she depends" (31). Religious practices can, of course, be rote. The self can be superficially present to its action. But a fully involving religious practice can produce a unitary connection between the brain, the mind, and religious believing. Again, credit the Spirit.

Given the billions of neural events operating within each person's consciousness, how can there be a unitary experience of the self on a given day and, even more remarkably, over the years? It is becoming clear that there is a loop between the neurons and practices. Benvenuti and Davenport's research shows how religious practices in particular enable a human being to come into a sense of being someone and belonging to something. The behavioral evidence for this seems to date as far back as the Neanderthals. Religious behavior seems to have been the ordinary way to go about being part of something larger and social. Had *Homo sapiens* known about the complexity of its brain before it amassed a degree of communality about living together from religious practices, one can only imagine how unsapiential we might have become, maybe even vicious.

The plasticity of the brain makes room for more and more learning. It also retains some kind of neural record of what it has experienced. The brain is in sync with the other systems in the body, like the limbic system, and sensory system and the executive capacities located in the neocortex. Without knowing how, human beings have usually been able to attain neurointegration. For the majority, it seems, this has been attained by religious practice. The religions have enabled *Homo sapiens* to believe that there is meaning, howsoever meaningless things might appear to be at a given moment.

This is not intended to be an apologia for the rightness of theism but a tribute to the innate ingenuity of humanity for its traditional ways of managing complexity and staving off the threats of harm, injury, meaninglessness, or death as the last word. The usual way this ingenuity has been operating and enacted and deepened is through worship in its multiple forms. Maybe we should salute the plasticity of our brains for what they have been doing over the centuries without their getting any credit for it. Neuroscientific knowledge is recent, but historically the sacred and the physical have been compenetrating one another all along. Only in very recent times has the neural purported to be its own explanation—as merely natural and adaptational. It would seem strange if after all these centuries there were no transneural meaning to religious practices or any sacred reality to which they were directed. *Homo sapiens* would begin to look like a sap, a duped, *Homo idioticus.*

The perennial testimony of the experience of the sacral need not be doubted, and can be confirmed because of recent discoveries about the neural role in worship. This information deepens our understanding of the components of the wholes humans have been able to experience and confect. Neuroscience helps us understand the orientation to transhumanism that has been "bred in our bones," as we used to say, but now we can more accurately see that it is bred in the head.

Transhumanism in one form or another is the aspiration to transition beyond ourselves. It is inherent in every human being. It has been scripted into humans' bones, neurons, and heart ever since the species *Homo sapiens* walked, thought, felt, wondered. How humans satisfy their aspirations for the *more* they seek will depend on their cultural milieux and on what social imaginaries they inhabit for envisioning their desire for this. *The new creation is such an imaginary.*

Physics in general and space-time in particular provoke transcendent-meaning questions. But the social imaginary of the faith(s) can supply such meaning. Whatever that faith is, it needs to be capacious enough to make room for further and further findings about nature. If physics or the sciences were to claim that faith and science are incompatible, they would claim to know something that is not knowable scientifically.

Some transhumanists are atheists. Atheistic transhumanists will probably increase if the believing community is content to be scientifically illiterate. Space-time information and faith should not be separate bodies of knowledge. Since knowledge about space-time had been unknown till very recent times, the understandings that naïve common sense had brought to afterlife as a *there* beyond space and a *then* beyond time, are goalposts that have to be moved. Our faith that there is an afterlife needs to take the new knowledge of these coordinates into account.

May 7

I want to argue for the connection between the Spirit and the neurons and the practices that act on values. Religious beliefs explain behavior, notwithstanding the many different articulations of who or what this Divine reality is. The issue of causality comes into play here. The simple way of understanding causality has cause come first, followed by effect. A more complex way of understanding causality now has multiple causes, like God and socialization and neuron and habit and all intertwined. Further rumination about causes would have to include memory, culture, mirror neurons. The testimony of countless generations about the sacred being the trigger and purpose of religious behavior is not refuted by the growing knowledge of the complexity of our present amount of neuroscientific knowledge.

Neuroscientists have been hotly pursuing this question of nexus between religion and the brain. Studies have been done on people who claim to experience God through contemplation or rituals or penitential practices, in group and personal prayer. These studies show the brain in overdrive at these times. The subjects of these studies have flummoxed those researchers who presumed they would be able to trace the explanation of prayer to one site in the brain or to locate "the god gene." In addition, the testimony of subjects to the meaningfulness of a life of contemplation is certainly not explained by those who would like to explain everything neurally. Since many of these practitioners of their religion name their experience in terms of the Spirit, this Divine Person needs to be recruited to see how resultant meaning and joy might be explained.

When asked about where they think the study of religion and of the brain is going, Benvenuti and Davenport say: "It is our expectation that cumulative neuroscience in the area of religion will show that ordinary religious practice brings about integrated neuro-circuitry that is distinct from ordinary consciousness but may be continuous with it and that such practices may also create neural networks for extraordinary religious experience" ("The New Archaic," 27). Even more venturesome is their expectation that "the key component of the neurological correlates of religious experience will be varieties of integration: integration of neurons and neural circuits . . . integration that individuals experience in cognitive and behavioral ways by feeling better and by creating a sense of possibility . . . and correlatively creating in the mind the subjective experience of meaning . . . [that enables] the placement of the self within the greater reality within which the self resides" (28). Their ability to objectively locate the loop between religious practices and the brain "may be a major building block towards a new religious epistemology constructed in a more complex style, and centering the performative and artistic" (32).

Implicit in their research that they have not articulated and as far as I know have not intended is that the psychological consequence of religious belief and practice might be a good reason for secularized moderns to revisit the value of religion. For human well-being, the reason for revisiting the issue of religion is that so many past generations have found meaning and community by believing in God and have found great value in acting on their beliefs.

But there is another side to the loop between practices and habits and the neural trigger. This is: <u>wrong practices and bad habits and how the neural can groove these into "have to do's."</u> The social consequences of these, beginning with the individual are not difficult to see, like discontent, abusive relations, addictions, etc. Paul would see these explained not by the neural architecture but by what he called "flesh," in contradistinction to "spirit" (Gal. 5:20–21).

To summarize several things we can now understand about the brain. One is that it is living. Two is that each brain cell is autopoietic. Each brain cell is one very small unit with membership in a vast empire of other cells, each of them doing its own thing but in such a tandem with each other that solo they would cease to be and that together they enable the living entity to be what it is. Three, the emergence of human life is a very small phenomenon measured over against the unimaginably large and long universe of living things. Four, how little we know. The mechanisms that explain the move from nonlife to life are not yet clear to us. Finally, most of the living things that are accessible to biologists have yet to be studied.

In addition to study, a further activity is possible to humans, given all this data about the brain. Gratitude. Gratitude for what? To whom? To the Lord and Giver of Life for those who subscribe to this belief. Why gratitude? Because if life is not self-conferred, it is a gift, and it has givers, multiple in fact. It certainly is an emergent, but as a phenomenon the explanation for it is not yet clear; hence the need to pursue more and more knowledge of it. That could be satisfying for the researcher. For those who don't have that luxury or training for study, the activity of gratitude is possible. Granted it is not an either/or; researchers can be worshippers, and worshippers can try to learn more about how the worshipped One "works."

May 10

A long time ago, around the year 375 CE, Basil of Caesarea understood the Spirit to be a connector or an interconnector or completer. Maybe "understood" is the wrong verb; "experienced" is closer to the mark. His praxis and that of his prayer community (his sister was in the vanguard of this energy), enabled him to come to a new understanding of the Spirit. Their praying brought him to an experience of a connection between humans and God that produced his theology. Technically, his own and his community's prayer was a discipline (a *lex orandi*) that generated his deeper faith-understanding: (a *lex credendi*). There was a loop between their prayer *praxis* and his pneumatological *theoria*.

The further context that moved Basil to do the theology he did were the disputes of his time in which he was embroiled. These were about the relationship within and between God and Jesus of Nazareth. Basil's pneumatology helped make their connection intelligible. Arianism had denied the divinity of Christ and of the Spirit, and it was winning the day. Beginning within the Godhead, Basil began to intuit that communion and being belong together, and that this should extend out to all reality. One could say that outside of the communion of being there is nothing, even God.

The theories of the sciences (relativity theory, quantum theory, string theory, chaos theory, systems theory) are trying to imagine how all that is now known is radically, foundationally interconnected.

Those who have expectations that some grand unified theory is still to be developed would be well advised to see that the seeds of such a theory were already sown in the fourth century and maybe just have to be watered for the long-sought-for Grand Unified Theory to be developed. Furthermore, these seeds might be able to flower in an unexpected way, and instead of coming up with a theory to control or gain the high ground of conceptual intelligibility, the Spirit could show the sciences what to expect from Its transconceptual, transincarnational, "blows where it will" reality. Pneumatology doesn't lend itself to objectification, the way understandings of Christ have, nor will a grand unified theory that is rooted in the Spirit. Pneumatology is the remedy for the felt need to grasp wholes through conceptualizations.

It should not be surprising that the Source of all the *creata* is the Trinity. It would be right, therefore, to connect the need for a grand unified theory to the character of the Spirit within the Trinity of Divine "Persons" where its role is as the connector. Divinity at its core is relational. The Greek for this is *koinonia*, so communion, wholeness, relationality. Being and relational and intelligible all go together. Outside of communion or the relational is nonbeing and unintelligibility. Ontologically and primordially whole is who God is. But oddly enough, and wondrously, too—where the Spirit of the Lord is, there is freedom (2 Cor. 3:18). Freedom to allow the Spirit to be the wind that comes from—God only knows where—and take one to—God only knows where! That's where the human Jesus got. He let It do a connecting he couldn't or didn't do.

May 11

To be even more specific than I was yesterday, Basil's pneumatology, and its relation to the brain as the latter is now being understood, should allow us to see the link between the brain's energies and the Spirit's energies. If the deepest insight into the Spirit was that it is a connector, it behooves us to try to see how Its uncreated energies are connected to the created brain's energies! The more cognitive neuroscience has unearthed about the complex circuitry of the brain, the more awesome the phenomena of brain and in turn the mind are.

Theology might also throw some further light on the amazing connections that we are now seeing between the neurons and neurotransmitters and the synapses and so on. Neuroscience seeks to understand this connectivity in its own way, but my way of understanding it is a traditional one. I think of the old adage "grace perfects nature." A more recent gloss on this has been accepted by much of the theology that has been beholden to Karl Rahner. That is that there is no such thing as nature *nuda*, if you will, nature naked. And further, there are different modes of the presence of God operating on every element and process and at every level of the material universe. Further, the Spirit is the immanent though largely anonymous presence of God in all reality. Much less anonymity is now called for since cognitive neuroscience has developed a sophistication about brain matter that doesn't explain itself or the mind or consciousness.

Granted, pneumatology is a difficult area to focus on. But of Christian theology's many specialties, the area of pneumatology (theology of the Spirit) is the one most germane to this question of knowledge and how it emerges from the brain. What has been found are energies. These now-known energies and the tradition's understanding of the Spirit's energies are the dots that need to be connected. Doing so should be of interest to those who delve into the mysteries of the workings of the brain, as also for those who seek more specific knowledge of how the mysteries of God operate in this small piece of creation.

I wonder too, whether the Spirit should now be seen as connected to the neurons and to the materiality of the brain as It has been thought to be to mystical graces? I believe it should! One way to understand the Spirit is as the energy of love, love of the true, of the good, of the beautiful, and more capaciously of every grasping of what is so, of what is real. It would seem appropriate to imagine energies going forth from the Spirit that can take in the whole arch of reality connecting God to us and us to God. It also seems that the Spirit's mission must be seen as including any and every grasp of reality as it is becoming known by humans as the Creator has been creating *La Realidad* all along. If this could be seen, the Spirit would be acknowledged, maybe even loved.

May 13

The Spirit's outreaching energies were imagined as both "uncreated" and "created" by the early Christian theological tradition, beginning with the Fathers of the church. These energies should be imagined as having a foot, as it were, in the uncreated and a foot in the created and, therefore, the neural. The Western wing of this Christian tradition preferred to theologize in the analytic mode with the category of "grace," or the graces. The more intuitive tradition of the East focused on the "energies," both created and uncreated, as they preferred to describe them. This latter articulation was formalized by St. Gregory Palamas in the fourteenth century.

Western Christians, in general, were rightly awed by the distance between the Creator and creatures and dealt with this distance by the idea of analogy. That was their way of ensuring that the knowledge that was acquired was only partly similar to and hence partly dissimilar from knowledge of the divine. Eastern Christianity, however, was awed by the synchronicity between the divine and the human. So it focused on the idea of the gradual deification of humans via the energies God conferred on them. The growing present knowledge of neuroscience should see these energies and the neurons as a work in tandem. We are not quite as transcendental as we might like to imagine ourselves to be. Nor are we simply understandable materially.

Once again the Spirit is able to be a connector between these two aspects of ourselves theologically.

The eleventh-century split between Eastern and Western Christianity and the still meager understanding of God by each grew larger as a result of the battle over "filioque." That doctrinal term carried with it the idea that the Spirit proceeded from the Father *and the Son* and proceeded from there to all of the *creata*. The East fought this filioque funneling, preferring to see the Spirit abiding in and resting on the Son, not proceeding from him. About this centuries-long argument, suffice it to say that the discernment of the mystery of God's relation to the world or of the Spirit's relation to all of creation would have been much more fruitful had it not been for the roiled ecclesial, cultural, political, and interpersonal antipathies about what the disputing parties were claiming to know at that time.

Without wading into the complexity of that historical dispute, it is good to recall that the masters of insight into the Trinitarian Divinity were the fourth-century Cappadocians, Gregory of Nyssa, Gregory Nazianzus, and Basil of Caesarea. They were representative of the Antiochene (Eastern) tradition of the Trinity. They would not have seen filioque as a legitimate inclusion into the ancient Nicene-Constantinopolitan Creed since that creed had been happy with the claim that "the Holy Spirit proceeds from the Father, who together with the Father and Son is worshipped and glorified."

I had been studying recent research about the brain when I received an invitation from the University of Geneva to speak there at a symposium on pneumatology. And the more I had learned about the brain, the more astonished I became about the complexity of this three-pound, between-the-ears organ, which I had been using all my life. Acquiring the knowledge did not produce instant piety—like learn a little about the neurons and then voilà see God as their Author. No, I am talking about hours of studying the data of neuroscience and its myriad ingredients and trying to figure out how the intricacy of the circuitry could possibly work. The more I learned, the more unlikely it seemed that such an infinite number of items could work in such harmony. It's like a thousand symphony orchestras simultaneously playing on key, in tune, synchronously. With no conductor in evidence! (For those who are amateurs but interested in the subject, see Carl Zimmer, "A Voyage into the Brain," *National Geographic*, February 2014.)

What follows is the presentation I made at the University of Geneva titled "The Brain and Basil of Caesarea."

I

Presently there is a vast amount of research going on in "this the century of the brain." Some of it is federally funded; some of it is more locally, university-financed. The competition between the initiatives is somewhat like the race to the moon some decades ago. Who will plant the flag of ultimate explanation on the brain? I doubt any of these research initiatives will, as long as it is considered a race that will be won by those who amass the most data. No, "the more, the merrier" empirically won't work! Rather, the more that is gathered, the more inexplicable the data seem to be.

So there is the matter of expectation. If the neuroscientist is working from a methodological naturalism, he or she will have an expectation that the brain will eventually be explained by empirical data accurately analyzed. But it is not incumbent on the neuroscientist to be a naturalist. By the same token, if pneumatologists ignore or overlook empirical data in their theological research, they will probably "find God," but in ways that won't do justice to the subject. And they are likely to be suspect for supplying "a god of the gaps" explanation. The Spirit and the empirical need each other.

II

3 lls

The brain has nine regions in it: the frontal and motor cortexes, the parietal, occipital, and temporal lobes, the corpus callosum, a thalamus, cerebellum, and brain stem. The regions are connected by 100,000 miles of nerve fibers called white matter. Gray matter is made up of our 86 billion neurons, each of which is distinctive, individualistic, idiosyncratic. Yet each does a similar thing in its minuscule locale. It is as if a neuron is monogamous, interacting with only one other neuron while the recipient is itself acting similarly with a third and on down the line. And I'm not even mentioning the axons and the dendrites, the synapses and the neurotransmitters, the chemical, biological, physiological, as well as the electrical ingredients that go into this "soup" that is cascading out into the findings of neuroscience. How this all could be is marvel enough, but that it works through its own interconnectivities rather than our intentionality is even more wondrous. What explained its emergence in *Homo sapiens* in the first place and now explains this neural functioning in billions of interactions in each present-day human being?

The first thing to strike anyone who finds out about the brain data that are being uncovered is the stupefying amount of it. The simplest brain, the lowly worm's, has so many connections that enable the worm to do its thing, that it looks Einsteinian. Present neuroscience breakthroughs involve the brain of the mouse and will take ten years before experts are satisfied they know how that brain operates. Meanwhile, the human brain is getting plenty of attention. All of these inquiries are aimed at figuring out how the brain functions—in the worm, the mouse, in me, and in you.

To discover how and why these connections are going on in the brain is going to need more than scientific information, invaluable as that might be. There must be something more connecting these dots to one another than all of the ingredients already mentioned. First of all, they are all alive and operating within an order with each part "knowing" what to do! I feel like a bystander observing a marvel, the beneficiary of something both ongoing and inexplicable. The biggest mystery is the interconnectivity of each of the parts. But then further connection questions arise: questions about the connections between the brain and the mind, consciousness and intuitions, habits, biases, beliefs, emotions, behavior, thoughts, etc. How do wholes get made? How do we become whole if we are made up of so many parts?

Incomplete is my feeling about this knowledge I have acquired about each neuron groping after something, one after another, and the whole lot of them (again 86 billion) vectored in an order that eventually produces my thoughts and affects and my behavior. There must be some explanation for all this that transcends their physicality and their individual and collective unidirectionality and rudimentary intentionality since within them they do not carry the explanation.

III

Connectivity questions, brain or otherwise, didn't begin with the sciences. To see how connectivity questions have been answered in the past and how the present data that is being discovered by these brain inquiries can be aligned with those past answers seems a worthwhile endeavor. Most connection questions were given faith answers. Faith stories are connection stories. One of these faiths is Christian.

Christian faith had its first act open on the primordial connection between the divine Spirit and the human in the scene of the Annunciation. The resulting baby, man, Jesus, was eventually believed to be the promised Messiah. Jesus' followers pored over the issue about the connection between him and God and his spirit and God's Spirit and that Spirit and them. The Christian belief is that before there is the human wherewithal to do any connecting there is a connector, capital C, the Spirit, who is the Enabler of all connectivity. The Spirit enables or provides people with the need and the capacities needed for connecting anything, like the brain and us, our minds and faith and the Spirit.

Basil of Caesarea, the fourth-century grandfather of pneumatology, was a connector, par excellence. In fact, for him, "the Spirit completes the divine and blessed Trinity" (page 63 of the *Hexaemeron*, which is a collection of nine homilies delivered by St. Basil on the cosmology of the opening chapters of Genesis). If the Spirit completes the Trinity, what does It do when it extends Itself to the economic order? The first book of the Hebrew Bible saw the Spirit as the mighty wind that "swept over the face of the deep" in Genesis 1:2 and began to bring order out of chaos. The Spirit is here supplying the wherewithal for making sense out of the otherwise inexplicable. So from the beginning the Spirit is playing the role of connecting everything that ever was, is now, or ever will be . . . beginning within the Trinity Itself. If the neurological doesn't have within it the wherewithal to explain interconnectivities, maybe the pneumatological might.

Basil was one of the three fourth century Cappadocian theologians (the two others were Gregory of Nyssa and Gregory of Nazianzus) who did the theological thinking that proved so fruitful at the Council of Constantinople (381 CE) when the Nicene-Constantinopolitan Creed articulated that "the Spirit is the Lord and Giver of Life." If that belief is true, the Spirit must be the source of the life of the brain. Neuroscience is unpacking the empirical foundation for this ages-old theological belief.

IV

It now seems as if each neuron is scripted with a kind of intentionality. Does this emerge from the physical or the other way around? Who knows? It might seem to be a stretch to stretch connection from within the Trinity Itself to all of creation and, in turn, to humanity and, in turn, to its most minute cranial parts, but doing so doesn't fly in the face of facts or any other explanation. What this outlandish claim that connects the Spirit with the brain and its interconnectivities might establish instead is an accusation about the massive ignorance humans have had—and negligence to boot—about acknowledging the part played by the Spirit in every one of the interactions of their living brains!

Knowledge of the brain and the Spirit, consequently, need each other both for a fuller explanation of each of them and of ourselves. *Without* the Spirit connectedness isn't, starting within the Godhead. *With* the Spirit connections happen "all the way down." Pneumatology has been inquiring for centuries about *what* God would have us know. But now with our new knowledge of the brain, we can see *how* the Spirit accompanies the most infinitesimal parts of the anatomy of the brain.

Scientism and empiricism as well as dogmatism and fundamentalism—all four of these *isms* have developed bad reputations, and deservedly so because each formally stops further questions and purports to be satisfied within an a priori, narrowed scope. Academic disciplines that aren't hungry aren't healthy. Healthy knowing seeks to go to ever fuller explanations.

V

All Jesuits undergo the Spiritual Exercises for their formation in spirituality. The starting point of these exercises has one reflect on "The Principle and Foundation," which states that each and every human being is created to praise, reverence, and serve God. Humans have lived for centuries before this particular moment in time, and all that time we didn't know much about the brain. Now we do. So my suggestion is to pause and praise God for this thing that is the brain, mine and yours—even if you don't want to extend that awe to the mouse's or the worm's, which are helping us know more and more about our brains.

The reason for doing this is that, if it is true that the Giver of Life which is the Spirit makes the brain breathe and has been doing so in every brain since there was a brain, the least we could do upon knowing this is to acknowledge the Giver. Great gratitude and praise seem called for. If for nothing else, the gratitude should be for the Spirit's utter "selflessness" for accompanying the countless number of acts in which our brains have been putting two and two together in the myriad ways we have ever since our life began. Yet few of us today realize that the brain is not the sole explanation for these completion processes!

Catholic liturgies conclude their Eucharistic canons with an exclamation of praise—to God the Father and his Son to whom "in the unity of the Holy Spirit all glory and honor is given forever and ever." But this unity making is not only intra-trinitarian; it extends beyond God to all creatures, which in analogous ways put two and two together. This paper suggests that this unity making and the intentionality of all living creatures should be noticed and their Lord's indwelling and working in them acknowledged! Where life is, there is the assistance of the Spirit enabling them to also be conclusive creatures in the myriad little ways and big that they do. The busy-ness of the bird outside my window and the intent of the evergreen tree to stay the course of being green—it belongs to those who see more than these do, to say Who it is that enables them to keep doing what they do.

This is not inventing a God to explain the gaps. Intriguingly, although the gaps in our knowledge of the brain are disappearing rapidly, one gap is widening: that is, what makes it work? As the extraordinariness of brain's activity becomes known, one is invited not just to marvel at its intricacy but to trace its living and functioning to a causality that transcends it and even our minds and our souls.

In short, there are five beliefs that, if subscribed to, would complete empirical brain inquiries: (1) What lives, lives because the Spirit gives it life. (2) The capability the Spirit imparts to the brain is connectability. (3) The actions of all the brains' ingredients are all in the direction of connection not autonomy. (4) The causality operating in them is not of a determining but of an accompanying character even at the most microscopic level. (5) This is not surprising if their cause is love.

May 21

The more neuroscience learns, the more it seems to unearth the same point: that is, the interconnectedness of everything. At least the "how" of it. The "why" of it is more interesting to me, but that is not neuroscience's focus.

For pneumatology to be a source of insight for neuroscience, it needs to be revisited in several ways. One is to develop more clarity about how the Spirit as a Person could or should be understood. Like Jesus and God, the Spirit has been believed to be a distinct Person. But all three Divine Persons are so only analogously to each other and to human personhood. But believing even that takes one only a short distance into intelligibility and underscores the character of unlike, which is the import of analogy. So the Person of the Spirit is as unlike Father and Son as it is like them, and all three are Persons like and unlike each of us.

Where the Spirit breathes, being is, and It breathes on each according to and as each is. The fourth Gospel and Genesis, the first book of the Hebrew Scriptures, both recommend seeing the Spirit as breathing or being breathed. So, in Genesis 2:7 God breathes life into all things, or all things come to be through the breath of God. The Psalmist sees the entire heavens and all their hosts as made by the breath of the mouth of the Lord (Ps.

33:6). On the night Jesus appears to his disciples, he breathes the Spirit into them (John 20:22).

The Spirit is preeminently God as immanent. We tend to be unconsciously anthropomorphic and individualist about God and Spirit rather than social and holistic. Just as our anthropomorphism has made us dangerous to the rest of living things, so also our cultural individualism has had us misread the mind of the writers of the scriptural texts about the Spirit's role and mission in effecting the interconnectedness of beings to one another.

One of the best pieces of evidence of the presence of the Spirit to human beings is their confession of God as "Abba" (Gal. 4:6). This name names the headwaters or the principal font of the mystery of God in creation. Another empirically accessible piece of evidence of the presence of the Spirit in persons is the tangible fruit of this presence in their interpersonal relations. For Paul these are: "love, joy, peace, patience, kindness, generosity, faith, mildness, chastity" (Gal. 5:22).

Since the Spirit as Sanctifier has been the preference of the doctrinal tradition for seeing the work of the Spirit, the sanctification of the elect had seemed like the preeminent achievement of the mission of the Spirit. It now seems right to also see the Spirit as the source of connecting everything to everything and, in turn, everything to God. The more data the sciences amass, the more relevant it seems to imagine the Spirit as Connector, Completer, the Interconnector of all that is. It would be ideal if the sciences come to the idea that the Spirit has a role in filling out their findings. Beginning with the Trinity and now including the sciences, communion seems to be central. Reality isn't ever going to be seen as a whole without this aspect of the Spirit being grasped. If all this sounds like repetition, so be it!

May 23

Recall the quaint picture of "the Lord God" taking a piece of clay from the ground and forming something unique and blowing into its nostrils "the breath of life so that man became a living being" (Gen. 2:7). The breath of God can help us understand the move from nonliving to living, from prehuman to human. "Spirit" in some way has been how human beings have been answering their special identity questions for a long time. The prescientific character of this picture does not make us ignorant to believe in it, any more than our scientific answers have made us wise. Both moments of civilization, the prescientific and the scientific, have developed from the same capacities of intelligence that ask and seek answers to questions.

The followers of Jesus had certain beliefs about him. First was that the Spirit came to rest on him and explained Jesus to himself, and then that the Spirit explained themselves to his followers. Further elaborations of this produced an understanding that was able to make a whole of God as Principle and Jesus both as his Son and as human at the same time. A triune God was gradually what Christianity concluded was the constitutive reality of the divine.

Another way of putting this is that the Spirit came into human consciousness functioning as a Unifier of what otherwise would appear to be unconnected, that is, humanity vis-à-vis divinity, or the Yahweh of the Jews and the God of Jesus. If this Spirit's role were to be seen as able to connect what otherwise appears not to be, then the work of the Spirit could be seen in the data the sciences are learning but which need to be connected better than the data are at present. Specialization is priceless but can be the source of endless separation.

What the early Christians came to see about Jesus of Nazareth was that he was not explainable unless the Spirit was what connected him to God. What they learned about him is something the sciences might also learn about the things of nature they are uncovering. The Spirit as connector could do for science what it did centuries ago for Christians' understanding of the Christ. Belief about him and his special connection to God has continued for all these centuries.

Another way of imagining this divine Connector is to start with where nature started, namely from the big bang and go from there to quarks to stars to planets to the formation of earth to living things to humans living. There are many ways of perceiving this flow, but one way is to see a connector behind each stage of the emergence of the universe to the next stage. Each new emergent depends on the old and on its component parts, but those parts and their connections do not have within themselves a sufficient explanation of how the subsequent one develops. Spirit should help explain both the emergence and the connecting of the prior stage to the subsequent one.

∞

May 24

As part of the Jesuit course of training I studied philosophy for three years in my early twenties. Although the courses were varied, the center of it was metaphysics. It didn't occur to me at the time that metaphysics is what everyone does, though very few do so formally. We all try to put together what arrives in our consciousness separately.

Brian Cronin's article "The Purpose of Metaphysics" (*Method* [Fall 2012]) is what got me thinking about this in relation to what I am doing in this volume. He claims that metaphysics is universal and cannot be avoided, although virtually no one knows he or she is doing it. What is it they are doing? "The real task of metaphysics is to unite and transform our knowledge, to promote genuine wisdom, to guide the pursuit of understanding in individuals, universities and cultures" (43).

There is a smudging of two things here. Although there are metaphysicians who formally "promote genuine wisdom and guide the pursuit of understanding," the rest of us implicitly or informally are metaphysicians just by keeping our act together or striving to make a unitary sense of reality.

I would add the Spirit to what Cronin describes as metaphysics. It accompanies human intentionality. I am not simply replacing philosophy with theology here. I am saying that all human intentionality has the Spirit present and acting in its activities. The brain is alive, and the Spirit is the source of its life. The operations of perceiving correctly or making the right judgments or reasoning and choosing are not self-explanatory actions of the self. The Spirit is an ingredient in all intentionality. Notice, an ingredient, not a determinant, since "where the Spirit of the Lord is, there is freedom" (2 Cor. 3:17). It should be obvious that the Spirit is not a determining ingredient since so many of our thoughts and choices are wrongheaded.

"We are all metaphysicians in a real sense and it is unavoidable" (Cronin, 27). I like Cronin's explanation of it, or as he puts it "the purpose and function of it." I want only to suggest that we are not the only agency operating in our minds and hearts. Metaphysics supposedly "unifies and organizes all our knowing" (35). Sorry, *metaphysics* isn't alone in this task.

I suspect Father Cronin, a Spiritan priest, would accuse me of leaving philosophy by my assertion about the Spirit, and that I would thus be violating the borders between philosophy and theology. I don't respect the borders. If metaphysics purports to organize all knowing, it has to include in its capacious embrace the knowing that faith in the Spirit produces.

It's not that one has to become a theological metaphysician to get there; it's that people are whole makers; they try to keep their act together; and the Spirit as the agency

at work in them is the explanation of this and why they act
this way, notwithstanding an almost universal inadvertence
to this reality.

Faith is not only reasonable; it can supply reasons reason
alone would never come to. Whole-making becomes difficult
when cultural dichotomies dictate boundaries, for example,
between faith and reason, theology and philosophy, the academy
and the unlettered, science and integration, church and state.
Whole-making becomes easier if there is a sufficient degree of
introspection to give an account of why we do what we do. So
here, are we the explanation for why we keep trying to make
sense of what doesn't initially strike us as making sense? The
Spirit is the reason why we are all little Aristotles, howsoever
incompletely, incoherently, implicitly our minds do that.

May 27

Somehow we have to explain the evolution of whole-making—
from the Big Bang to the littlest bangs at the subatomic level
to the human level all the way out to the ends of the universe.
I would suggest a whole-making cause helps to explain such
diverse effects that are obviously at the same time unitary.

The Spirit has been accompanying the workings of nature
in the entire course of its evolution. This is asserted not as a
proof, but as a belief. The Spirit unfortunately seems never
to have been in a rush to be recognized, and, sure enough,
its presence has largely gone unrecognized. Both the Spirit's
accompaniment of evolution and recognition of the Spirit Itself
seem to be mirror images of each other—that is, slow.

A transhuman causality has been believed by our human
ancestors from the earliest time, as archaeological, anthropological, and historical studies of their worship practices have
continually unearthed. How primitive of them! But the findings

of modern science also invite the same recognition that there must be something more than materiality, and more than human operating both in nature and human nature.

This will be more easily seen by scientists if there is a willingness on the part of theologians to be engaged with and informed by what science is learning about matter, that is, that there's so much more to learn about it than we ever imagined. But there is also so much more to religion. Furthermore, science and religion have something to teach each other. Neither, of course, will have anything to learn from the other if the practitioners of each are satisfied to stay within their own fortresses of knowledge.

Matter was perennially seen as inert and able to be shaped only by something immaterial, like form in Plato, or entelechy in Aristotle, or soul in Western Christianity, or the energies of God in Eastern Christianity, etc. The shapers were multiple in the history of civilization. Philosophy's denigration of matter to its place of relative insignificance was helped by Descartes's dualism. He posited two mutually exclusive ontological categories—res extensa and res cogitans, material stuff and thinking being. If that were true, the Spirit could only qualify under the category of and in the realm of res cogitans, mind, and thus would not be able to account for its interconnectivity with and between and in all res extensa, material realities.

In a sense the debut of the personhood of the Spirit in history began with Jesus' Last Supper discourse. Jesus speaks of the Spirit in personal terms even though Its personhood was unlike that of any other person the Twelve could have imagined.

Even though God has been understood as three-personed, with each in the genre of person and on a par one with one another, understanding the Spirit as Person is more complex than understanding the Father or the Son as Persons. The Divine Persons are not in relation to creation in the same way. Wind, fire, breath, water, and oil are all part of the metaphoric ways that the revealed texts speak about Spirit, but these do not convey personhood as easily as the names Father and Son do.

Christians confess that all things were made *through* the Word but are much less clear that it was *in* the Spirit that all living things came to be and still come to be. There is one divine nature, but there is a proper role for each of the three Divine Persons vis-à-vis creation. The simple attribution of creation to God has made it seem superfluous to see the distinct and proper roles of the Spirit in creation as also those of the Son and of the Father.

An example of this distinctiveness of roles is the relation between the Spirit and truth that Pope John Paul II quotes in his Encyclical, *Fides et Ratio.* "All truth, from whatever source, is from the Holy Spirit" (#44). Thomas Aquinas recorded this belief (*Summa* 1–11, 109, q 1 ad 1). But the author of this insight was neither John Paul nor Aquinas but Ambrosiaster, a fourth-century, pre-Augustine theologian. The assertion: all truth, from whatever mouth it is uttered, if it is true, is from the Holy Spirit. Whatever is true whether seen faintly or clearly, has as author the Spirit. I would prefer co-author. Cognitive neuroscience does not speak of truth as such, but this fourth-century assertion invites our connecting the neurons and the Spirit.

Since the Trinity is One, one can become lazy, and speak of the One God at work in all that God has made as if God were not Triune and undifferentiatedly doing the same thing, and acting the same way. The oneness of God remains true, but there is a role peculiar to each of the Divine Persons. Further insight is needed into their unique roles, as the Scriptures suggest.

The Spirit's unique role in giving life to what lives and to the evolving uniqueness of each living thing does not exclude the role of the Source of the Origin of Life, Abba, or Father, if you will. Nor does it exclude the belief that it is *through* the Son (Col. 1:15–20) that all things living and nonliving are made.

What needs to be said and seen and believed is that the Spirit is immanent in this interaction between Creator and creature. The Spirit is the immanent Life-Giver. The Spirit is poured out, pours "itself" out with something specific "in mind" in each of Its givings, so that the living thing poured into becomes itself and in turn is connected with the communion-of-Persons that is the Trinity. The bestowal of the Spirit is in function of each entity being in a real relation to each of the Persons of the Trinity with a view to all eventually being in a relation of communion one to the other.

The Spirit's presence, though largely unnoticed, can come to be known to every human being. The Spirit can connect life known, as it is becoming known in its most recondite forms through the sciences, with the eternal life to which all of things living are vectored.

Without its being able to name it, all of nature awaits the glory of communion of finite beings with the Infinite Supreme Being. So the Pauline invitation to his hearers was to see glory as nature's future, each creature beyond mortality and in full union with its Creator. All of the sciences could see their data in light of the law of the Spirit which is for *doxa*, glory, for "the glory to be revealed." "Then the world itself will be freed from its slavery to corruption and share in the glorious freedom of the children of God" (Rom. 8:21).

The eschatology of Paul, and the "finalities" intrinsic to nature, and the data of the natural sciences all have more to say to us. They can either stay separate or they can be connected. Even the lowly neuron has its role to play in this interconnecting. Human adoption into the family of God is mediated through living neurons and both are known through the life-laden Connector Spirit.

Like the neutrino and the neuron, the Spirit acts as a go-between, enabling humans to know what God would have them come to know, beginning with their own intra-psychic groanings. These groanings produce language which is traceable to the cerebral cortex which overlies the two cerebral hemispheres. But even when we do not arrive at distinct knowledge, the Spirit helps us in our weakness both in our thinking and in our praying. This assistance enables one to keep on thinking or praying. And God takes up where the Spirit, notwithstanding all our forms of weak praying leaves off, and "knows what the Spirit means," which is not as praiseworthy as the would-be knowers or pray-ers say or know or mean (Rom. 8:27). What the Spirit knows is that all of creation has one similarity with praying humans, and is eagerly awaiting the revelation of the glory, the same thing the children of God await (Rom. 8:19).

May 29

One of the things that still bedevils me about the Spirit is the question of name. Is the Spirit's name "Spirit"? It's comforting to know that Jesus' name is Jesus. It makes him more familiar. And so often in Scripture and theology and Church teaching, the "name" given the Third Person of the Blessed Trinity is "The Spirit of God." Though it is an identifier, a descriptor, it doesn't sound like a name to me, a personal name. Yet Person is what we are talking about and the One we are addressing when we pray for or to the Spirit. Yes, the Spirit of God differentiates the Third Person of the Trinity from the Father and the Son, but does it name that Person?

I am not aware of any place in the Gospels where Jesus addressed the Spirit like he did the Father, though he had much to say about the person of the Spirit, especially in the Fourth Gospel. In all four Gospels he addressed God as Father, his and ours. So what to make of this name question about the name of the Spirit?

In the Old Testament the Spirit could not have been conceived of as a Person largely because of Israel's monotheism. Such a differentiation within the Godhead would have been inconceivable. Yet in Matthew 28:19, when Jesus commissioned the eleven to baptize those who would come to believe in him, he instructed them to do so "in the name of the Father and of the Son and of the Holy Spirit." Was this transmitting to them the name of this Divine Person? This doesn't necessarily follow from the baptismal formula itself because "the Son" was not Jesus' name.

Several comments on this baptismal formula in Matthew are salient. It almost certainly conveys the practice of the early Church which was being done for those who became Christian. It is surprisingly Trinitarian and egalitarian—Father/Son/Spirit. So we have here three Divine Persons long before the theology of Trinity was worked out. The formula is a unique theophany in and of itself since it conveys the human Jesus in his divine milieu, something unimaginable to Jesus in his lifetime, but consonant with what we come to know about the post-resurrection Jesus. The baptismal formula that his followers use says more about the Oneness of God than it does about the Spirit's name. This baptismal commissioning scene is redolent of Jesus' own baptism scene where, as he emerges from the water of the Jordan, "suddenly the sky opened and he saw the Spirit of God descend like a dove and hover over him. With that, a voice from the heavens said, "This is my beloved Son, My favor rests on him" (Matt. 3:16–17).

But did Jesus believe at the time of his own baptism that the divine favor which came to rest on him was a Divine Person, Spirit? I very much doubt it. But in the much more mature fourth Gospel, he used the term *Paraclete* to describe the Spirit. For example: "I will ask the Father and he will give you another Paraclete who will be with you always: the Spirit of truth" (John 14:16–17). But the Paraclete names the role of the Spirit, not the name of the Person of the Spirit. The Paraclete was believed to be an advocate for those persons who were baptized in Christ. The Greek *parakletos* means an advocate for, or "someone who is called to the side of one in need of assistance" (*McKenzie Dictionary of the Bible*, 636). Furthermore, Jesus calls the Spirit "another paraclete," with Jesus having been the first one, so the Personhood of the Spirit is not named by Jesus; Its role is.

"If I fail to go, the Paraclete will never come to you, whereas if I go, I will send him to you" (John 16:7). By the time of the fourth Gospel, the Spirit was a person to the Evangelist. So, again, whether Spirit or Paraclete, do we have a personal name or only what the One sent is sent to do?

Maybe I am expecting the wrong thing, since the Spirit in contrast to Jesus is not incarnate in the sense of a single, humanly accessible person. The incarnation of the Spirit is in a sense in many persons, in as many persons as have been baptized in the name of the Spirit and maybe countless more whose lives have been led by the Spirit unbeknown to them. So it might mean that the communion with God which one is being baptized into is name enough for now, until the communion which is the mission of the Spirit is final and the end point of Creator and creation is fully attained. I wonder what we will name the Spirit then? Maybe love!

One more thought: maybe everyone who is led by the Spirit is how the Person of the Spirit chooses to be named. That would be a lot of names. But that might go along with the degree of self-emptying that the Spirit operates with and from, as we have already seen.

June 2

I think the most revealing moment we have about the agenda of the Holy Spirit in creation can be grasped in the scene of the Annunciation. The Angel Gabriel announced to "a virgin engaged to a man whose name was Joseph of the house of David" that "the power of the Most High" would come upon her and that she would give birth to a child who would be called Son of God by all those who would subsequently be drawn into believing this about Jesus (Luke 1:27–35). This Annunciation event reveals the Spirit's agenda that had been operating from the beginning of creation and will continue until God is "all in all." What is it? To make wholes where otherwise there seem to be just separated parts. The whole here was the union of divinity and humanity beginning with the blastocyst that formed in Mary's womb. The best way to understand the Spirit's work in the world is to see the Annunciation as the biggest neon billboard the planet will ever see about the Spirit's mission.

What started with Mary and the Spirit continued with Jesus himself, because he was Spirit-filled, and he kept putting together wholes from parts. He took the law that pharisaic Judaism taught and placed it in the larger panorama of love, for example. Or he saw the disdained Samaritans in a way that his hearers didn't expect when he singled out a Samaritan in the parable of the good Samaritan. Even more obvious was his making people whole by his healings (a fifth of the Gospels are filled with healing stories). In a word, his entire mission in his lifetime might be described as whole-making work. And even more intriguing was the way the Spirit led him, little by little as far as we know, to make into a whole his own developing self-understanding of God's relationship to him. With the Spirit's assistance he was able to weave together the large messianic dreams Israel dreamt with the pathos of the four Suffering Servant songs. He was inexorably brought (kicking and screaming?) into seeing that he was the one who would make these two contraries of Servant and Messiah come together in his own person.

What the Spirit is about is leading us into the same whole-making within ourselves, one another, people, and cultures. With the assistance of the Spirit, we have further dots to connect or architectonic wholes to put together in our understandings and by our actions. Like death and life!

June 4

There's no end to the work of confecting wholes of what isn't delivered to us wrapped that way. I have in mind two examples from science. One is taken from the Human Genome Project and a subsequent one that calls itself "Encode." In 2003 after $3 billion had been poured into the research about it, the human genome was sequenced for the first time. Before their sequencing, we had learned how each of us is a network of genes, some 21,000 of them. But this sequencing only provoked further inquiries because there was more that was left unknown, because 98 percent of the genetic material had been dismissed and given the inelegant descriptor "Junk DNA." That "junk" has now been found not to be peripheral at all but a very active and essential part of our genetic structure.

So the first breakthrough that produced the sequenced human genome has now yielded up a vastly more complex whole. The Encode project, which has been in the making since 2003 and cost $185 million, published its findings worldwide on September 9, 2012, in a coordinated production of thirty papers in multiple scientific journals. As with the genome project, it was as if we were viewing the data from outer space, but now with this most recent Encode project, it's like we have been able to zoom in on every street in our bodies and can actually see the traffic moving.

More specifically, Encode has learned that there are some 400,000 regulators or enhancers operating between the genes, which keep them, as it were, operational. So instead of ignorance or the presumption that there is something like a biological desert between one gene and another, we now have access to the intricate interactions and the ingredients that control when, where, and how gene behavior works. The amount of raw data that has been uncovered from this Encode project is already estimated to be in the area of 15 trillion bytes. To imagine this, someone has suggested we generate the image of a room with a 52-foot high ceiling that extends for 18 miles. That conveys the innumerable "parts" that we now know operate in each person. Each person is a whole, but so much more goes into our being whole than we ever imagined before. We are each a whole, independent of the choices we make or the food we eat or the relationships we have. These 21,000 genes and 400,000 "regulators or enhancers" are how each of us is alive and one. Unbeknown to any previous generations of humans we are now able to be knowledgeable about our genes and our neurons and all these interactive ingredients that go on within and between both of these.

If the ancient Psalmist could exclaim how we are wondrously made, how much more should we be able to do so now! Now that we know these things, can the science that has unearthed them subscribe to this belief and explain the marvel that we are? Can it explain the harmony that obtains from such multiplicity and complexity? Or: what enables the zillion little parts in each of us to function as one, insofar as we do almost in spite of ourselves? I want to suggest that this genetic and neural information is revelatory in two senses. One, in itself; two, about how the Spirit puts together what would otherwise be separate. The more we know about our physical makeup, the more we should see how inexplicable we are if there isn't a whole-making something effecting and explaining us to ourselves and one another.

New scientific information might be able to evoke in us the need cited in the passage from Matthew 13:52: "Every scribe who is learned in the reign of God is like the head of a household who can bring from his storeroom both the new and the old." We need to put the new information with the old. For us who are made in the image and likeness of God, God's Spirit seems very invested in having us see wholes that previous generations couldn't have imagined.

We tend, of course, to put the new information in a box, and keep the older faith information in its own storeroom, apart from it. But this doesn't do justice to God and to the responsibilities of a learned scribe, whose knowledge has to integrate the old with the new. Otherwise the scribe becomes "so yesterday" and never takes on the role of the head of the household.

Integrating the old with the new is not a job for the fainthearted nor for the weak of faith or mind. To undertake the task is to take up the work of the Spirit whose mission is to make wholes that otherwise stay unknown. To undertake whole-making work requires the assistance of the Spirit. Knowing that this assistance is there and asking for it is to ask for wisdom. Putting all of these pieces together is what makes one a faithful scribe.

June 6

It seems that most of the new things we are learning come from science. But that should make the old ways of God new to us. Like what? (cf. Frederic Parrenin of the University of Grenoble, "Synchronous Change of Atmospheric CO2 and Antarctic Temperature," *Science,* March 1, 2013; Vivi Kathrine Pedersen and David Lundbek Egholm, "Glaciation in Response to Climate Variation," and Simon Brocklehurst, "How Glaciers Grow," both in *Nature*, January 10, 2013). The last ice age ended with the sharp increase of carbon dioxide in the atmosphere. That gas is considered by scientists to have a most negative influence on the health of the earth, on its temperature to be more specific. So this knowledge of the planet's ill health we scribes can and now must bring out of our storeroom and connect it with the growing knowledge we already had—namely, that the use of fossil fuel (gas, coal, oil, etc.) by us humans since the beginning of the industrial revolution in the eighteenth century has been warming the planet perilously. There has been a 41 percent jump in the carbon dioxide produced by humans since then. This could produce an increase in sea level around the globe of 25 feet or more, "albeit over a long period."

Since each of us in little ways is contributing to the warming of the planet, those of us who aspire to be good scribes must try to make a correlation between our personal faith identities and this new scientific information. How to make the link with personal habits and one's religious habits? First, by letting our praying be informed by knowledge of the intricacy of the world's designs.

One's personal prayer need not be any less personal the more informed it is. It is not just between God and me but between God and me as one recipient of the knowledge that the natural sciences are unearthing. These findings uncover the minute empirically discovered ways of God that can now complement the ways of God that the Bible has taught us.

This way we ignore neither the old nor the new and can make a whole out of them. That would be a way to do justice to the mission of the Spirit. It is obvious that *Homo sapiens* has been brought into a whole new degree of responsibility as our species learns more and more about new dimensions of reality, like carbon dioxide gas . . . its plus (the ice age shrinks and we emerge) and its minus (we're ruining our planet by our use of fossil fuels) . . . and our responsibility (to stop it). In a word, it is now an urgent necessity to see the centrality of humans to the future well-being of life. This new knowledge unmistakably conveys the fact that the whole of nature works together or doesn't and begins to become undone—because obviously 'together' it *isn't*. For shame on our species that is undoing nature!

To whom does this new knowledge (and action taken on it) make a difference? (1) It makes a difference to those scientists who are looking for something more than science alone is able to do. (2) It makes a difference to those whose knowledge of science is scant, but whose faith knows that it has to be open to new findings and their connection to faith. (3) It makes a difference to those who teach one of the scientific disciplines or some form of theology or religion because that can show how a religious tradition might be able to give an account of itself and at the same time stay *au courant* with where knowing is going. (4) It makes a difference to those whose responsibility is of a liturgical or a catechetical nature so that they can convey a faith that has the character of *aggiornamento* to it. (5) It makes a difference to the Spirit and to Its mission of truth. (6) It makes a difference to the earth's well-being to make a whole out of parts, here the sciences and the faiths. Finally, it makes a difference to God that those made in his image and likeness awaken to the fuller meaning of their calling as humans. We are part of the warp and woof of the rest of nature and to its future well-being or ill-being.

June 8

As already mentioned, some ten years ago I began a study about how researchers in academia go about the process of doing their work. I concluded very simply that they were aggregating the data each had access to. They each come up with very different aggregations from the particular questions they posed from the data available to them in their fields. I found each of them construing distinctive wholes from parts they could access.

I connect the indwelling Spirit with this whole-making that I now see we all seem to do. Even species other than us do.

When did evidence of ingenuity begin to show itself in history? The first thing I think of is Jane Goodall's research on chimpanzees. She spent much time with them, studying their behavior and found it remarkably prescient in the literal sense of that term. For example, their use of tools. The chimpanzee knows how to take a twig and insert it into a termite hole and withdraw it so that it can eat the many insects on the twig. This is ends/means "thinking." They are envisioning something beyond the object itself, and they make use of a tool to fulfill their needs. It is envisioning a whole from the parts of hunger, twig, termite.

I think too of the hominid, *Homo heidelbergensis,* who 500,000 years ago put two and two together and made a spear to throw and puncture the flesh of an animal. How did it "think" that up? Perhaps by association with its own flesh being torn by a thorny bush. At least this is the idea that the cognitive scientist Liane Gabora contributes to the answer. She then proceeds to seek an explanation of the move from associative thinking to analytic thinking with an assist from dopamine and other neurotransmitters firing up creative thinking the way *Homo sapiens* does.

There have been no new hunts for an explanation of innovation and creativity. It seems to me that one ingredient explains this same penchant as it appears in all living species which do the same thing. In short, they put together parts, and this precedes *Homo sapiens*. It even precedes hominids. What explains this even though each species stays within the range of its own capacities? Might the Lord and Giver of Life be the source not just of life but of the innovation and creativity so many species display?

An example of very early sophisticated cognition was bedding unearthed two years ago in South Africa dating back

77,000 years. What was found was a tribe who had achieved knowledge of the vegetation in their area, in particular, of leaves from a particular kind of tree that had natural insecticides; when the leaves of that tree were made into bedding, the mosquitoes were kept at bay. This tribe lived by a river, and their health depended on the connections they learned. In this instance, they learned that these leaves were naturally able to kill bugs. This same tribe also learned how to make multi-ingredient glues that fastened pieces of wood together for fashioning tools and constructing their dwelling places. Chemistry, here we come!

Other researchers have unearthed the tools of a hunter-gatherer tribe, which lived some 90,000 years ago; the tools were devised to tailor animal hides into clothing for themselves and to make red ocher paint for their artistic enterprises. This pigment was made from abalone shells. An even earlier species, *Homo erectus,* learned how to kindle fire for warmth and protection from predatory animals (cf. Heather Pringle, "The Origins of Creativity," *Scientific American*, March 2013; she is a contributing editor for the journal *Archaeology*).

What does all of this data say about innovation or creativity that preceded our species? And what explains the gradual emergence of "cognition" over time? It seems that there is some degree of ability in created things to make wholes out of disparate parts. But what explains this? A number of the sciences—e.g., anthropology, primatology, neuroscience—have weighed in on supplying an explanation. Cultural ratcheting, and increased brain size and much analysis of the different levels of cognition all have made a contribution in explaining how hominid species evolved in their associative, analytic, and technological capabilities. One level of cognition is meta-empirical. Mathematics and concepts and hypotheses and intuitions and big dreams—in a word, thinking out of the box—all need to be explained meta-empirically. Is "thinking outside the box" explained by what's in the box? Yes, partly. No, fully. One explanation of innovative thinking is that God makes stuff with the ability to make *or* unmake itself.

The Spirit whose mission has been operating since life began has evidently been operating more fully in the cognitional life of humans. Their centuries-old belief is that that their species is more similar to God than all the other species. But innovation had many prehuman predecessors. Those species began to show signs of being able to think outside the box, even though humans "take the cake" in doing this. The Spirit as an explanation is not submitted for apologetic reasons or as a proof that *Homo sapiens* is made in the image and likeness of a divinity who has been believed to be the Creator of all beings and their capacities. It's just that this explanation explains more about innovation—humans' and prehumans'—than any other explanation yet devised, it seems to me. Innovations are "chips off the old block" that is God.

June 11

Augustine and Aquinas described the mission of the Son as visible and that of the Spirit as invisible. The invisible mission of the Spirit needs a philosophy of interiority. Lonergan's understanding of how subjectivity becomes authentic is a valuable one for laying out such a philosophy. He elaborates two paths of development, one upward (through a succession of "inner words" achieved through experience, understanding and right judgments and from there to values) and one that is downward (an outer word that is articulated through a tradition handed on through values and beliefs). This outer word has sources, teachers: Scriptures, authorities, traditions as well as nature, as science finds out more and more about its workings. The findings of science can become inner words, as this text has suggested.

experience + Tradition

All Tradition has come from experience
Much experience has come through Tradition
But not all experience comes through tradition.

A Biography of the Spirit 85

However they are described, there is a dialectic between the inner and outer word. We need the two missions, and thankfully have them, one of the Spirit and one of the Son. In history the upward or Spirit mission came first, and the downward or Christ one came second. There is a necessary interrelationship between these two words and the two missions, and the two Divine Persons. One's heart can be flooded with love, but the loved reality needs to be named. Unfortunately, one can use the words of faith without one's heart being in it. Religion can become rote, with someone being satisfied with going through the motions of faith unfed by the inner word.

June 12

The Spirit can be very self-effacing: "There is a notable anonymity to the gift of the Spirit." Fred Crowe speaks of Jesus' three self-emptyings. There is his ontological one (he emptied himself of his divinity), his psychological one (he grew in his human consciousness), and his historical one (he was of then, of his culture and time). I wonder whether there might be three self-emptyings of the Spirit along the same lines—ontologically, psychologically, and historically. An emptying into living creatures who each strive to "think outside of the box" for their own survival or well-being (as mentioned before). Into all of these strivers, the Spirit is emptying Itself. It has to conform to the nature it accompanies; It has to conform to their minds in the analogous ways; and It has to take up Its accompaniment in the particular history of the creatures it assists. So each Spirit-assisted moment contributes to the whole development of each creature. To narrow this down to one species, _Homo sapiens_, one can see how an integrity in one's interiority affects one's relationships and even one's culture positively, and conversely how inauthentic subjectivity is a source of confusion in a culture. Writ large, inauthentic subjectivity generates wrong thinking and wrong choosing, and eventually ideologies that are culturally disastrous. But an authentic subjectivity is able to get to objectivity and to the well-being of the person in his or her immediate surroundings. So viewed from below, the Spirit is self-emptied so that all might be filled.

June 14

Steven Weinberg, who has been awarded a Nobel Prize in physics as well as the National Medal of Science, is a master of his area of knowledge. His stature in matters of science is sufficiently prestigious to take his words about its limits seriously. In "Physics: What We Know and Don't Know," an overview of his field written for the 50th Anniversary Issue of the *New York Review of Books* (November 7, 2013), he admits that many of the hopes that physics has had for breakthroughs have not materialized and that we may have to be content to accept that. As he puts it, the number of things that can be explained "may be fewer than we thought."

His modesty comes in part because he realizes that the character of the observations and speculations of the best of scientists about physical reality are inevitably limited by human "anthropomorphism," which he realizes can be "crude." He's not denying that remarkable discoveries have been made, especially in the last fifty years, in both cosmology and in knowledge of elementary particles. In both cases widely accepted "standard models" have been produced.

He is also very specific about the limitations of our knowledge in two areas. One is about dark matter, so called because it doesn't emit or absorb light. Its existence is inferred rather than empirically located; inferred to explain the fact that clusters of galaxies in our universe "hold together gravitationally, despite the high and random speeds of the galaxies within those clusters." Yet "no one knows what dark matter is," even though it is believed to be "fully five-sixths of the matter of the universe." A second area of limitation about the mystery of matter is about the expansion of the universe. Weinberg comments on the discovery made in 1998 by two astronomers about this, in particular that the universe is expanding more rapidly than had been previously realized. But this has been explained by positing an energy previously unaccounted for by any of the rules of particle physics. Hence a whole new dark has been imported into the picture to make sense of this new inflation information. "Dark energy," which is just as mysterious as "dark matter," is the name given to explain these otherwise clear computations.

To make wholes out of parts in their respective fields, science has at times had to posit beliefs about things well argued for and arguably real, but not seen and for the most part inexplicable. Like here: dark matter and dark energy. These are asserted because they are needed to complete the understanding of what is empirically verifiable. Both of these "darks" are hypothesized in order to complete the picture of previously unknown aspects of the universe.

But what we have come to know is that most of what we have learned is that we don't know, leaving us in the dark about the universe and us in it. Pneumatology is a completely different field or discipline from physics. It is also up against a huge unknown, huger in fact about what is known about It than the universe. Pneumatology's unknown is the Holy Spirit. But the irony is that the two things that keep being emitted from this unknown are light and energy. And the more light and energy that is emitted by the Spirit, the more meaning we are able to come to, personally and collectively. And meaning is what the other two darks don't give.

The wisdom of the Spirit has been what most believers have had recourse to as a source of light over the centuries about the Divine Dark. And this Spirit has had suppliants seek the energy they've needed to pursue the good and to come to knowledge of the truth. What explains this continuing recourse to the wisdom of God over the centuries? Is it merely imagination or the experience that it pays off?

Although the mysteries of matter and energy will continue to be pursued so as to try to reduce their darkness, the suggestion here is that the energy and light the Spirit can supply, as It has over the centuries, can assist the Weinbergs of the world, present and to come, in uncovering more information about these two darks and furthering the understanding of the meaning of *Homo sapiens* and *La Realidad*.

The assumption that physics and pneumatology are apples and oranges and shouldn't be mixed is being scorned here. The pursuit of truth is one and the same and has been throughout history. And the end result will eventually be that truth is one. The promise of Jesus in giving the Spirit was that It would lead us to all truth. The light and energy of the Spirit can only help in trying to pierce the darkness of matter and energy and ignorance.

June 16

I have been revisiting the Spiritual Exercises, through the lens of one of the key meditations in them—"On the Contemplation to Attain Divine Love." The grace the retreatant is instructed to ask for in this exercise is "for an intimate knowledge of the many blessings received, that filled with gratitude for all, I may in all things love and serve the Divine Majesty." The response to these blessings besides gratitude is that one make oneself available to God to do with them what God wills, and thereby to "praise, reverence and serve God and by this means to save one's soul."

Invaluable as the Exercises have been for four centuries, and continue to be for so many, the way God's will was understood then is not the same as it is now. Recall that this famous little text of Ignatius Loyola is methodological, not doctrinal. So present-day readers and pray-ers can see God's will differently than Ignatius had understood it while being disposed to going where the same Spirit led him and would lead them via his method.

We know so much more about nature and about our interdependent relation to it and hence about our relationship to God than Ignatius could have known. We have mortality in common with all things living. The preferred way to interpret this in much of believers' pasts was to believe in some form of afterlife in some place that wasn't here, e.g., heaven, or into a radically opposite condition, e.g., hell. This positioned the status of nature as useful for our getting from here to the better of these two theres. The resurrection of Jesus from the dead presaged the way to get beyond the confines of nature and away from it to an up there where the saved souls dwell.

Not so fast, says Paul! He was sure that "the whole world eagerly awaits . . . [what we await] and [that it] will be freed from its slavery to corruption and share in the glorious freedom of the children of God" (Rom. 8:19–21). Pauline thinking invites one to contemplate one's kinship with nature that is in the same condition of mortality as humans are in. All of it is mortal, and lives hoping "for the glory to be revealed in us" and all creation (Rom. 8:18). How and when and through what will this "glory" be revealed? Paul would contend that it is already being revealed in those who have the experience of the Spirit, though even in them it is only in a "first fruits" degree of knowledge or manifestation.

So does this tiny population of the already-knows have anything besides their claimed experience of the Spirit in common with the rest of mortal creatures? Yes! This tiny population has what the rest of creation needs, namely the fruit of the Spirit, which is hope. Not hope that sees clearly into the future but hope that accepts not seeing into the character of this afterlife and experiences hoping for it and entrusting oneself to God now.

This Pauline vista rearranges the chairs on the deck, and would have one believe the boat we are all on is not the *Titanic*. Was Paul right? If Adam had a chance to speak, he would confirm Paul, and if Noah had a chance to speak, he would too. Adam would say: I was settled by the Lord God in the garden of Eden. My commission was to cultivate it and care for it and enjoy it (Gen. 2:15). And Noah would say God established a covenant with me and all my descendants as well as "with every living creature that was with you" (on the ark) (Gen. 9:9ff.). God promised to enfold all of them and the human species together in this covenant bond "for all ages to come" (v. 12).

I believe that covenant puts a new spin on our world vision. God has made a radical commitment to creation by creating it, and an even more profound commitment to what he created by covenanting with it. Embrace is covenant's primary connotation; so the vulnerability displayed in and by this divine posture is nothing less than astounding. It is right up there with the incarnation of the Second Person of the Blessed Trinity in how it provokes a very different way of seeing God than the precovenantal ancients or their religions could ever have imagined. To put it graphically, it is as if God is saying, "I'm not satisfied with just being me, so until and unless you and your descendants and all nature that has been revived since the flood are in communion with me, I won't rest."

The self-emptying of the Godhead in the Incarnation is wondrous. But the category of covenant should have the same scope as the embrace initiated by God to the parties to whom it has been extended, that is, "to every living creature that was with you, Mr. and Mrs. Noah." God needs the embraced believers to be not only with God, but for them to include in their circles what has been included by God in covenant: "every living creature" (Gen. 9:10).

June 22

Only one divine intention has been operating in all of Scripture: it is covenant. Realizing this should deepen an understanding of God as intent and single-minded throughout the passage of time . . . was yesterday, is today, and will be the same forever. No divinely initiated covenant has been revoked, annulled, or retracted by God. Covenant took many forms over the course of Israel's history. We would have considerably more knowledge of God if the meaning of covenanting could be grasped. We could know that God is a recidivist, that is, keeps falling into this same habit.

It is interesting to see how during the Old Testament's evolution, Israel's understanding of covenant moved from externals to something more interior and interpersonal, interdivine/human, and eventually trans-Israel. The Sinai covenant was written on stone tablets. The new covenant was/ is written on hearts. The old covenant required charismatic leaders and prophets to teach and exhort the people how to live according to elaborated stipulations. In the new covenant the promised Spirit would teach each person in their hearts how to think and do and be. The new covenant, furthermore, was not offered to one people, but was to be a light to the nations. Before this universality took hold, Yahweh established a covenant with David and his household. And the Divine Partner in this covenant promised that if the embrace was yielded to, the result would be eternal.

It has always been the Spirit that made covenant experientially available to human beings, though their experience seldom involved an awareness of Spirit as such. The Spirit's accompaniment of the operations of consciousness slowly enabled human beings to develop an understanding of themselves and eventually even of understanding itself. Earlier generations needed instructors to come to a greater sophistication about their interiority, but little by little, people could find their own critical and appreciative capacities developing.

From the beginning of human consciousness, transcendently real knowledge that has been unearthed by archaeology was named in many different ways. For Christians, the Spirit is the source of all these religious experiences. Vatican II's claim is that "the Spirit is at work in the heart of every person, through the seeds of the word, to be found in human initiatives—including religious ones—and in mankind's efforts to attain truth, goodness and God himself" (see John Paul II, *Redemptoris Missio*, #28).

June 24

The Spirit makes a We where the language and stipulations of covenant can make it sound like an *it*. God and I and you and all who are covenanted to God. Covenant needs to be the foundation of ecclesiology. Without Spirit inspiring covenant, Church can get stuck in an "it ecclesiology" and lose its grip on the divine-human-nature unity that grounds it. The degree of God's investment in covenant could not be more vividly manifested than Jesus' saying, "This is the new covenant in my blood."

Blood is the most tangible ingredient in the act of God's covenanting. Blood was understood as the life-force in the perception of those who were being invited into covenant. A ritualization of human covenant often had both parties to it—the offered and the offerer—sprinkled with blood. This signified, in effect, that they were one blood, even more intimately, one family. The blood of the earlier covenants with Yahweh was from sacrificed animals. But in the New Testament, the blood was Jesus of Nazareth's. His was a commitment in blood to his followers.

Transfusions of blood are life healing, can even be life saving. Transubstantiation in the Catholic understanding of Eucharist is that wine can become the life-healing, life-saving blood of Christ for those who partake of it in that setting. Transfusion and transubstantiation both have the prefix *trans* in common. While much technical knowledge went into the development of the technology of blood transfusion, there has not been much development of theological knowledge about the transmission of Jesus' blood to humans. An insight into how this can or might be understood will come from reflecting on Hebrews (9:11–14). In a rich tangle of imagery and symbols the author there asserts that "the eternal Spirit" was the agent who made the transition from the old covenant to the new possible. And in disentangling some of these images and symbols I believe we can learn how the cup of wine can become the blood of Christ.

The passage sees Jesus as high priest entering the sanctuary of the Temple once and for all. He enters and passes through it not by destroying it but by sublating it. His own blood is poured out, not the blood of a sacrificed animal; he is now the way worshippers are cleansed. How could this transposition happen? "The blood of Christ through the eternal Spirit offered himself up to God unblemished." So what does this mean for the rest of us? The covenant had a migratory element to it. It was always initiated by God but took various forms. Covenant started with the one made with Noah and then with Abraham and Moses and David, though none of these three ever rescinded the scope of the first one which was with Noah and his descendants and all mortal creatures. Like all before it, the new covenant was to deliver transgressors from their transgressions. It delivers "all who are called." Those who hear the call and respond to it will have their consciences cleansed and receive "the promised eternal inheritance" (vv. 14–15) through the Eucharist.

There is a double agency going on here, Christ's and the Spirit's. Most of the attention has been given to the former, not the latter. But it was "through the eternal Spirit" that Jesus offered himself to God. And it is through this same Spirit that we, and "our works," in particular the work of right thinking and good choosing, are pleasing to God. Insofar as "our works" are authentic, we are acting in the image and likeness of a thinking, choosing God.

The Spirit assists our believing the wine is the blood of Christ, and our sinfulness makes consuming it necessary. We know our "robes" need to be washed frequently "in the blood of the Lamb." And the Spirit keeps us hoping that his blood was poured out for all of us to make us worthy of communion with God's holiness now and for all eternity. And "this hope will not leave us disappointed because the love of God has been poured into our hearts through the Holy Spirit who has been given to us" (Rom. 5:5).

What I am saying is that the role the Spirit plays is multilayered. It accompanies the operations of the subject insofar as it moves from subjectivity to objectivity. It chides consciences when they are self-invested rather than self-transcending. It assists the mind and the will in the direction of the true and the good. These movements go on *modo humano* and gently though they can be done *modo abrupto* and bring one up short by commanding one's attention. Intercession is a further description of the Spirit's role. "The Spirit makes intercession for us (to God) with groanings that cannot be expressed in speech" (Rom. 8:26). Finally, and most importantly, there is the Spirit's causality enabling one to act in the direction of faith, hope, and love.

June 30

The ultimate mission of the Spirit has been to bring about a union between humanity and divinity. When Mary was told that "the Holy Spirit will come upon you and the power of the Most High will overshadow you" (Luke 1:34), the secret was out in the open. This initial whole was completed when Christ through the eternal Spirit offered himself unblemished to God on Calvary (Heb. 9:14). But the Spirit had been tying the shoelaces of humanity to divinity long before the Annunciation and Calvary. But now we have a paradigm that is easier to understand since Mary's yes and Jesus' self-emptying and his having taken his seat at God's right hand.

A brief biblical retrospective seems called for here to see the mission of the Spirit's assisting authentic intelligence to produce right order through right thinking and choosing. Like ourselves, our biblical forebears operated within a dialectic between faith and reason. They had to understand their faith and to also have faith in their reasoning. The authors of Genesis had two ways of understanding the role of human specialness among the *creata*. The first was that humans were made in God's image. The second was that they were to be the gardeners responsible for the *biota* and *abiota* they themselves were embedded in. They saw humans mandated to till the garden by caring for it and growing it (Gen. 2:15).

The most obvious evidence we have that we have not appropriated this second image of gardener is our presumptive superiority over the rest of the *creata*. And the best evidence we have that we have not appropriated this role of our humanity is that we seem to have become the most destructive species that has ever emerged from the soil. Notwithstanding our remarkable technological prowess, we are still tillers of soil and drawers of water. We are tethered to the soil from which we have come and to which we will return. That's not the whole story, but our negative consequence on the earth is the most overlooked part of it.

Again, the first way Genesis saw human specialness was that humanity is made in the image of God. The God of the Scriptures was a covenanting God. We should therefore look more closely at this divine behavior to understand in whose image and likeness we were made. We were made to covenant. But at the same time Genesis ranks us as on a par with all the other existents. We emerge from the dust and clay of the ground (the *Adamah*).

We have much evidence both from the Hebrew scriptures and from our own experience to believe that we are of earth. There is a dialectic in those scriptures—Paul named it: we humans are earthen vessels with a treasure somehow embedded within this earthiness (2 Cor. 4:7). Both/and: as mortal as earth and as eternal as God.

So although living things are emergents from the soil, dirt, dust, and clay of the earth, when the Spirit is sent forth, all earthen things are renewed. The Psalmist saw the Lord "giving food in due season" to all the biota; "when You give it to them, they gather it up; when You open your hand, they are filled with good things." Even more at the core of their living, God was seen as the source of their breath, and "if You take it away they die and return to dust" (Ps. 104:27–30).

Job's friend Elihu put these same dots together in the same way. "The Spirit of God has made me and the breath of the Almighty gives me life." Even more remarkable: "it is the Spirit in a person, the breath of the Almighty that makes a person understand" (Job 32:8). Elihu connects the dots the same way the Psalmist does: "God, create in me a clean heart; give me a new and steadfast spirit; do not take your Holy Spirit from me" so that he will be able "to teach transgressors your ways" (Ps. 51:12–15). One wonders whether we will be able to return to these simplicities and see faith and reason as equally dependent on God's Spirit.

Israel awaited a deliverer, a messiah, who would have its cause in his mind and heart, and would be successful in carrying out his mission. What will he have going for him? The Spirit will rest upon him and will give him "the spirit of wisdom and understanding, the spirit of counsel and might, the spirit of knowledge and fear of the Lord" (Isa. 11:2). The noetic character of these gifts, both in Job and here in Isaiah, should be noticed! Also notice they are not political or military or economic or seemingly even religious. They have to do with knowledge—knowledge that includes: wisdom/understanding/counsel/power and all of these with full awareness of the otherness of God, hence "fear of the Lord." Furthermore, this messiah will learn that it is too little for him to be concerned with only Israel. His light is meant for all the nations. Light in two senses, one that the denizens of the nations will come to understand what they have to understand for their well-being and their progeny's. And two, light to understand their dependency on God for producing knowledge, especially saving knowledge.

The Hebrew Scriptures themselves attest that the Spirit of God did not appear for the first time in human history at the Annunciation. It was there all along in human intentionality but only occasionally acknowledged or—as with the prophets—so intensively present to be named as the source of their understanding. Jesus of course adds considerably more light to the reality of Spirit, its personhood and mission, but it had been present to life from the beginning of the life's emergence on earth.

Jesus person-ed the Spirit of God, distinctively giving It a personhood not previously perceived. The role and name that Jesus gave to the Spirit was Paraclete! It is a term not used in the entire Septuagint. As was previously mentioned, in Greek it means "someone who is called to the side of one in need of assistance." The scriptural variations in the English translations of Paraclete hint at the different ways this assistance is given: Comforter, Counselor, Advocate, Helper, Accompanier, or Company-keeper.

Jesus promised his listeners that the Spirit would assist them, especially when they had to deal with their adversaries. They wouldn't have to prepare a brief for their defense. This point merits attention and enlargement. What if these adversaries included their own biases, cultural and personal, social conditioning, their blind spots? In other words, the Spirit's assistance would not be limited to times when others were their adversaries. The Spirit could then be seen as assisting one's subjectivity in dealing with adversaries that were within one's own consciousness, and this makes the movements of the Spirit harder to discern.

It should become evident that the Spirit has its own "mind." One of the best records of that mind in the New Testament is the Book of the Acts of the Apostles. It describes a community continually challenged to keep up with the pace of the Spirit, who always seems to be running ahead of them. Jesus promised them that the Spirit would lead them into "all the truth." He assured them before his departure that they had many more things to learn, not the least of which would be about this pervasive presence of the Spirit leading them (John 16:7). Peter in particular seemed to have had a penchant for putting boundaries on the Holy Spirit's actions. It took him a long time to learn that this Spirit freely blows where it wills, ahead of where Peter wanted to go. After the Resurrection he was warned by Jesus: "As a young man you fastened your belt and went about as you pleased; but when you are older you will stretch out your hands and another will tie you fast and will carry you off against your will." John then adds that this was "the sort of death by which Peter was to glorify God" (John 21:18–19).

If one were to believe the Scriptures about the Spirit, then our present humanity in its best moments, that is, its right judgments and choices, like those of the past humanity of our forebears could be acknowledged as accompanied by this Spirit treasure, which has been embedded in rational animality from the dawn of light. That would help us see how dependent we are on this Holy Breath breathing into us and into our intentionality and not getting ahead of us, but assisting us with Its breath.

July 1

Two areas of the science-theology dialectic could be made more fruitful if a connection were to be made between the Spirit and the brain's processes. A theology of cognition needs to be developed with the data of cognitive neuroscience.

For starters, since the Nicene Creed professes a belief that "the Holy Spirit is the Lord and Giver of Life," that should have us see the Spirit operating in human intelligence, hence in all the operations of one's consciousness. But would the Spirit be absent from the emergence of those things that preceded human life and the life of minds? All of which is to say that the event of Pentecost should be seen as the occasion for the Spirit being acknowledged as a Person and named and celebrated more pervasively, rather than as making Its debut in history at Pentecost. The Spirit is the Lord and Giver of Life and therefore of the long process that it took for life to emerge.

Even if one doesn't believe in the Holy Spirit, everyone looks for some explanation about their personal experiences of coming to *aha* moments or insights or little epiphanies or to conclusions that don't seem to be fully explained by one's own efforts. One explanation of these experiences could come from many who have testified to a "more" in their knowing that they say comes from more than themselves. I am referring to the huge population which has been naming this "more" as a supernatural reality, howsoever they have named this.

One reason why Spirit has not been sufficiently noticed in the course of previous centuries as accompanying us is that too many Christians have believed that only Christians receive the Spirit and, even more narrowly, that only some of those chosen souls do. This is far too tribal a perspective and contributes to the neglect of the Spirit in modern understandings of understanding.

July 3

Again, I want to go back to Romans 8:19–27 because it is a wonderful text for gaining insight into the mind of Spirit. The passage sees all of creation groaning for meaning and recommends our noticing that we too are one with these groanings. So our experience of incompletion is enfolded within the wider swath of all of creation's own aspiring and hoping. And, voilà, there is a third groaner: "the Spirit himself who makes intercession for us with groanings that cannot be expressed in speech" (Rom. 8:26). So, each creature in creation is not groaning alone but is accompanied each in its own way by this co-groaning Spirit.

We have the Spirit, and we still groan. Paul makes sense of this in four ways. One is that we have the Spirit in a first installment only. Two, that this makes all of us together hopers. Three, we don't even know what it is that we are hoping for. Finally, that we are always seeking more understanding than what we already have. Human groaning has a unique character to it that differs from the rest of creation. We know we continually seek to know.

Paul focuses on our overall experience of "weakness" as thinkers and choosers and, in particular, as pray-ers. He sees the Spirit's role as assisting us with these weaknesses, with sighs that help us give birth to the words we utter and undertake the deeds we perform. Our "prayer," such as it is, is not particularly knowledgeable about the large picture, since we neither know what to pray for or about or how to pray (v. 26). But the One who searches the terrain of hearts makes sense of it because God "knows what is the mind of the Spirit," whom Jesus calls our Advocate (v. 27). What a comfort it is to think that the Spirit completes the groaning that our praying is.

To put this scene in Trinitarian terms: God the Father accepts the weakness of the one who prays. Not only accepts our weakness but accords humans a part to play in the completion of the cosmic mystery of this God-world-human species interrelationship. God the Spirit has been operating all along to give humans a part to play in what is always still becoming. And finally, God the Son would then be seen as the midpoint between the alpha of the big bang and the omega of the fullness of the kingdom of God. Humans can then be seen as agents of this drama of creation itself.

Some of the other statements Paul makes about the Spirit give even more dimensionality to this co-groaner role. (Paul did not write treatises; he wrote ad hoc letters to ad hoc communities about ad hoc situations.) His discernment and experience saw the Spirit as "a searcher of everything, even the depths of God" (1 Cor. 2:10). So the Spirit who knows "the things of God" (i.e., the character, or the ways, of God) knows that things are still unfolding (maybe even to God). Paul's asides seem to invite our imagining God as patiently waiting for us through our words and deeds, to complete the final pleroma. This in contrast to the Greek and scholastic notions of divinity as perfect, complete, as having already arrived, so to speak.

It would, of course, be too presumptuous of us to know whether imagining God-as-becoming is true of God or not. What is not presumptuous is to expect this mystery that is Emmanuel, God-with-us, to continue to unfold and surprise as it does. A static divinity, a got-it-made-God is not what the groaning of the Spirit suggests. Paul's earlier pneumatology anticipated John's later one, which has the Spirit leading the followers of Jesus into *all truth*. There isn't a contradiction here. One truth we could be led into is to getting a sense of how love has both parties, in this case one divine, one human, take their cues from one another, and in this sense maybe God becomes!

(manifests, expresses, ...

July 6

The best way, of course, to understand anything about God
is through Jesus. In particular, seeing Jesus as letting himself
be clay shaped by the hands of the Spirit-potter. Certainly,
without this potter the clay would neither have been the shape
it became nor would it have been accepted by God as "ransom
for the many." Jesus has been the most trustworthy witness ever
since, of this concinnity between the divine and the human.
Although it happened centuries ago, he is still who he is, and
they are as they are.

It's not that the New Testament's pneumatology was wholly
new. It's rather that the Ruah (Hebrew) of Yahweh had not
been sufficiently named or personalized within the mystery of
the Godhead before Jesus and his human experience of God
made this Third Person known. Jesus himself was groaning
(Mark 7:34) as his own incarnate personhood emerged. He
only gradually experienced his own communion and sonship
with God as Father with the help of the Spirit.

All of which is to say that humans are not alone in their
groaning. As was said, there are three such: the Spirit and
ourselves and nature. And God "who searches our inmost
being knows what the Spirit means" (Rom. 8:27). We and all
creation are profoundly partnered with heaven. Because of this
we should naturally go from thinking to thanking. This way
"the God who searches hearts" would to some degree complete
our incomplete groanings.

Like the first communities described in Acts, Paul himself
had a hard time keeping up with the freedom of the Spirit. His
pneumatology gives several indications about how he saw the
Spirit's uncontainability. He connected it with the "charismata"
(1 Cor. 12–13). He saw the Spirit as the author of these abundant
differentiations. In Romans 12 he speaks of the Spirit's activity

not in terms of the proliferation of these charismatic gifts but as renewing the mind. Renewed reason produced results that became a "living sacrifice" that glorified God.

Paul experienced his own reasoning being assisted by the Spirit. For him "renewed minds" come to judgments that are "good, pleasing and perfect" (Rom. 12:2). Their insights then are not arrived at by themselves alone, or solo. Paul also makes explicit the doxological character that is latent in human knowing. He suggests that Christians need to offer themselves as a "living sacrifice" to God because of and with their renewed minds. This is neither recommending that they think more highly of themselves or their thoughts than they deserve nor that they think of themselves as wise (vv. 3, 16–18).

He is not naïve about thinking, his own or anyone else's, since he knows how it can fall prey to darkness. Or according to the more classical formula, although our intentionality is always moved *sub specie boni*, what we are moved to could in fact only appear to be good. His experience was that humans are up against biases that are not always of their own making and that their own unassisted intelligence is likely to be culturally conditioned. But by its fruits this dark source can be detected. From "flesh" disgorged from the Spirit come enmities, strife, jealousy, anger, quarrels, dissensions, factions (Gal. 5:22).

If one does not have any sense of or appetite for pneumatology—and few seem to—one might ask oneself how to explain the amount of discord experienced in domestic, civil, political, and religious communities and in all interpersonal relations. Paul would not see these as inevitable or as sufficiently explained by socially mediated influences or as intrinsic to human relationality. He posited something adverse to the human authenticity operating in us and in our milieu and personalized this adversarial thing as sin. Sin in both the Hebrew and Christian scriptures is personified evil. Beginning in the mind, it takes wrong leads, then gets to wrong doing.

However, Paul also posited a contrary principle in those whose lives manifested choosing and doing the right thing. That principle was named in different ways by him: the law of God, or the law of the Spirit, or simply the Spirit.

July 8

Obviously, the word and the work of the Spirit have varying degrees of detectability or sometimes almost audibility.

In a Jesus or even a Paul they seem to have been most audible. Jesus' ability to name the mystery of God in terms of the endearing name "Father" has warmed whole civilizations for centuries about the benign character of God. And Paul's comment that no one can claim Jesus is Lord without the assistance of the Holy Spirit has had the confirmation of millions.

The Spirit's assist is with both faith reasoning and reasoning itself, which allows consciousness to be not preempted but assisted. One could complain that the Spirit is too self-emptying since Its sighs, which are "too deep for words," have been coming to the assistance of humanity from the beginning of the development of its subjectivity. If assistance to humanity hadn't been largely overlooked, we could have continually been offering our minds and hearts "as a living sacrifice holy and acceptable to God, your spiritual worship" (Rom. 12:1).

The reason for the Word's becoming flesh was to enable humanity to attain further and further degrees of glory. The first installment of the Spirit is not just a pledge or a promise but is the actual Spirit given so that this glory might grow in time and history. This accompaniment of the Spirit is more than a promise, it's an already begun kind of thing. One can be transformed from one degree of glory to another by aligning one's own aspirations with the Spirit's aspirations, which are for truth. The Spirit's assistance is present in us so that we can be grasped by God's glory. Awareness of the Spirit and also of this (glory) doxa obviously admits of degrees.

The Spirit does not accompany human beings to make a sect or separate tribe, but a whole of all and of all creation. The Spirit is given to renew individuals and their minds with a goal to eventually "renew the face of the earth" with the new creation. It is given to contribute to the development and solidarity of humans with humans and humans with earth, and the whole of this with God. The more freedom the Spirit has to move in subjectivities and the freer subjectivity is to let It, the more the common good will be realized. Insofar as the followers of Jesus can come to see, as he said, that "those who are not against us are for us" (Mark 9:38–41), the more the renewal of the face of the earth will have a chance to take place.

July 10

What hasn't been sufficiently taken into account by contemporary pneumatology is the relationship of the Spirit to the realm of epistemology. And since that relationship has been overlooked, as far as I can see, I will develop that direction briefly here.

The best starting place for the connection between Spirit and epistemology is the transcendentals as notions. These notions are the primordial orientations in human intentionality that get concretized by insights, concepts, ideas, theories, and so on. I imagine the Spirit is the source of these, supplying human epistemology with its orientations, notwithstanding our inadvertence to either them or It. Then I want to connect this direction of thinking to the more recent religion-science dialogue in neuroscience.

Plato (429–347 BCE) introduced the world to the notions of the good and being and the true and the beautiful that were already operating in everyone. These transcendental notions are what we are oriented to if we can see deeper into what we hunger for. These notions for being and goodness, truth and beauty are like the engines that move us, sentinels on the lookout for what is promising, subliminal passions that seek particularity. The notions are hungers just below the surface of all human intentionality. They keep getting satisfied bit by bit.

Aristotle (384–322 BCE) picked up where Plato left off but did so a bit more arcanely. The notions for him are "concerned with the universal characteristics which belong to the system of knowable reality as such, and the principles of its organization in their full universality" (A. E. Taylor, *Aristotle* [Dover, 1955], 18). This is abstract, missing the concrete ways we have of always seeking and finding, always in particulars. Our hungers are for truth and beauty, goodness and being, and we are satisfied if only for the moment, and then desire more of same.

The Spirit is foundational to the insights of Plato and Aristotle, as well as to those of Jesus and Paul. The human spirit and the Holy Spirit and the notions all fold up into one inextricable ensemble of desire. Their extrication and differentiation can be enlightening about the self, God, and knowledge.

One of the best of the extricators of these notions has been Bernard Lonergan. His insights into them whets my appetite to connect them to pneumatology, though that is something he doesn't do. Just to take the notion of being as Lonergan understands it. Obviously, we all have a desire to know and to know purely in the sense that we don't want to fool ourselves or be deceived by what we think we know or want to know. Even before we know whether something *is* or *is not*, we have the desire to know which is the case. The notion of being precedes and extends beyond each known. The notion of being is prior to thinking; it is prior to concept. The notion of being, therefore, "must be the immanent, dynamic orientation of cognitional process. . . .

Desiring to know is desiring to know being. . . . Thinking is
thinking being; it is not thinking nothing; but thinking being
is not yet knowing it. . . . Judging is a complete increment
in knowing; if correct it is a knowing of being" (*Collected
Works of Bernard Lonergan: Insight*, ed. Crowe and Doran
[University of Toronto Press, 1992], 378).

"The notion of being is all-pervasive: it underpins all cognitional contents; it penetrates them all; it constitutes them as
cognitional" (380). Prior to all the contents of cognition are the
notions. Prior to answers are questions, and prior to questions
is the notion of being. "Experiencing is only the first level of
knowing: it presents the matter to be known. Understanding
is only the second level of knowing: it defines the matter to
be known. Knowing reaches a complete increment only with
judgment, only when the merely experienced has been thought
and the merely thought has been affirmed" (381).

All peoples have a spontaneously operative notion of being.
Theoretical accounts of that notion will differ according to the
philosophy articulating the particular account. The notion of
being does not determine which account is correct, "it merely
determines that the intelligently grasped and reasonably
affirmed is being" (385). There is no end to the meanings that
come out of being.

All of this stuff about being can be turned into the meaning
of matter and not just the matter of meaning. "As the notion of
being underpins all contents and penetrates them and constitutes them as cognitional, so also it is the core of meaning"
(381). Our thinking is not vacuous; it is purposeful, interested,
intentional.

The Spirit is given by God to help us in our obvious weakness,
not only with prayer but also with understanding. The capacity
of the mind to transition to truth beyond the question—as well
as beyond hunch, bias, conditioning, socially mediated ideas,
self-interest, and emotions—into verifiable knowledge is not

assured. I am not suggesting that the Spirit is supplying the knowledge. That would be a needlessly interventionistic or an adventitious idea and one that is contrary to our experience of slogging toward intelligibility and meaning.

Lonergan's insight into the notions and their relation to subjectivity is very helpful. He sees us as needing to be obedient to these transcendental precepts. Here are his four imperatives: be attentive, be intelligent, be reasonable, and be responsible. Notwithstanding the world's inadvertence, I believe it is the Spirit that assists us both in this obediential process and with the notions. The Spirit's sighs evidently move one in the direction of being attentive, intelligent, reasonable, and responsible. Since coming to knowledge usually is hard work, we are likely to imagine ourselves as alone in its pursuit. My suggestion is that we take the dots connected by the forebears of our faith, which are testified to in Scripture, and connect them ourselves. By doing so, I end up with the Spirit of God accompanying human intentionality.

∞

July 12

"Praise the Lord from the earth, you sea monsters and ocean depths; fire and hail, snow and ice, gales of wind that obey his voice, all mountains and hills; all fruit trees and cedars; wild animals and all cattle, creeping creatures and winged birds, for his Name only is exalted, his praise above earth as in heaven" (Ps. 148:7–10, 13).

What is our relation between our praying and their "praying," each in its own peculiar way (e.g., sea monsters) of praying? We can be their mediators to God both because of our reasoning and choosing powers but even more so because of our priestly character. According to the New Testament, all who have been baptized are baptized into the one priesthood of Christ. As such they are empowered to be mediators between "heaven and earth." But before Christians Israel had a priestly role mediating between the divine and the created. Israel itself was called "a kingdom of priests" (Exod. 19:6), and the Christian community picked up from there and saw itself as a "royal priesthood" (1 Pet. 2:5).

Nature praying! "The heavens are telling the glory of God and the firmament proclaims his handiwork" (Ps. 19:2). If from nature there is declaration and proclamation, why should not the priestly people hear it and join in their declaring the glory of God?

"Day pours out the word to day and night to night imparts knowledge" (v. 3). Each day tells the next day and each night the next night the knowledge they need to be day and night and the next day and the next night—how enriching to see this; how dumb to miss these outpourings.

"Not a word nor a discourse whose voice is not heard; through all the earth their voice resounds and to the ends of the world their message" (v. 4). How stupid it would be to go through life deaf to what all the earth is speaking; how much better to enter into rejoicing at both their speaking and our hearing them.

"He has pitched a tent there [on the earth] for the sun, which comes forth like the groom from his bridal chamber and like a giant joyfully runs its course" (vv. 5–6). A personified sun is acting like a lover who emerges in the morning from the tent or bridal chamber. "At one end of the heaven it comes forth and its course is to the other end; nothing escapes its heat" (v. 7).

The Spirit of Christ into which the baptized are consecrated can make these connections that otherwise seem bizarre and unconnectable. The baptized can enter into the liturgical action that has been going on continually between the heavens and the earth since time began. To join in and even be mediators of this cosmic liturgy are advantages the baptized are meant to enjoy. As mediators between the divine and the human, they have been baptized into the conjunction of Jesus' two natures. Nothing else in nature itself, nor even in human nature, has the same calling and power the baptized can exercise.

It must be disappointing for God to have his Son become one with human nature and his Son's followers become small—small in the sense that they lose the scope and sense of prayer that the Psalmist was testifying to. The Psalmist didn't imagine that liturgical prayer began with him. The world of nature is the world where liturgy begins and has been continuing ever since there was nature. The baptized have something very important to bring to it—the ability to tell nature what it is doing. How absurd it is to constrict the length and breadth, the height and depth of nature's praying to an anthropocentric parochialism.

St. Ignatius recommends in his Spiritual Exercises that the retreatant ask the grace for the intimate knowledge of seeing God dwelling in all things. I am thinking of an even more specific grace, namely to see God operating in the things of nature and that just by their being what they are, to see them praying. Our mediatorship supplies what is wanting in their praise, namely intentionality. And their praise and praying might even supply something wanting in us.

Nature itself needs humans to receive this grace as much as we humans need to. Imagine what would change if we could become as broad-minded and large-hearted in our prayer as the creation and the Creator are. The Spirit would teach the connections and interconnections between the things on the planet and us. We need this grace in order to celebrate in and with creation. These connections can be more easily made if the praxis of our worship is seen as joining in with what nature is already doing without its being able to name it. Nature loses by worshipers not seeing nature praying—and vice versa.

July 14

I think of the vision Peter, James, and John beheld when on Mount Tabor. Moses and Elijah are seen in a cloud of light conversing with Jesus. The transfiguration scene says something about physics (Matt. 17:1–9). Space-time has never been more disarranged. Einstein could have been bemused by the way space and time are conflated here. The time of Moses, Elijah, and Jesus are simultaneous and in the same space-time. The transfiguration invites us to expect more from our senses and perceptions than they usually deliver, and to learn that we can see further than we have seen. And in the final take "they look up and see only Jesus" back into the commonsense experience of space and time, of here and now, but informed that there are more layers to the real than the here and now.

The figures of Moses and Elijah are significant. They symbolize the law and the prophets. Their simultaneity with Jesus completes the troika. The whole event disobeys common sense about space and time and invites a sublation of them. The law and the prophets were in communion with the new law and its prophet. This is not only a transfiguration about Jesus but also an epiphany about space-time. For us, a used-to-be can be present in the now. The fuller *now* is what is being revealed here.

Space and time are matters of experience, whereas space-time is a matter of theory and knowledge of theory. Space-time is, of course, a unique kind of being, but so is anything else about which *is* can be predicated. Was there a time when space-time was not? Is there a space or time when it will not be? I don't know if there is a clear answer to these questions. In general, communities of people of faith have posited a creator for an answer to explain what came to be, and have posited what they will be in the future. Just as space-time has not been seen but has been explained, so too describing it as created is an explanation.

So a theological explanation of space-time is put forward to contribute a meaning to it that goes beyond the empirical for those whose worldviews are as wide as the wide lens of created/creator. Being able to find layers of meaning beyond the empirical doesn't deny the character of that material layer, but it gives more explanation than can be found within it.

All of this brings up the issue of sacramental knowledge. The principle of sacramentality has been employed by human intellects as far back as human knowledge goes. It sees reality as able to communicate the presence of the sacred. So seeing something more in space and time or space-time is a stretch only for those for whom the principle of sacramentality is unfamiliar or bogus.

Sacramental thinking is more likely to develop because of the experience of the sacraments. The bread and the wine are believed to be the body and blood of Christ for many Christians. The water and the oil can be more than water and oil for the same population. Sacramental thinking is used to seeing more and learns to hear a voice and enter into a time that is eternal while still in time. "Amen, amen, whoever hears my word and believes in the one who sent me has eternal life" (John 5:24).

Reality is diaphanous to the child. The price of adulthood can be an opaque realism that narrows its expectations for betterment to science and technology. Sacramental knowledge is knowledge. Science keeps overcoming ignorance. But the gains of science do not eradicate the need for meaning. They may in fact increase it. If one needs meaning, one needs faith in something more than scientific data so that what is not seen can come to be known. Then, too, what was believed can be seen to be either ignorant or seen more clearly. Seeing something that the sciences wouldn't know in the light of faith produces faith knowledge. And faith knowledge is real knowledge.

Otherwise, the overwhelming majority of the human race, past and present, would have to be judged delusional, deluded, or just plain stupid. Experiencing the immensity of space and imagining the eternity of time and the conjunction of time and space are ways of taking in reality and one's own mortality and maybe even positing God as a needed ingredient for their explanation and meaning.

Death?

July 18

I find myself reflecting on space-time in connection with prayer. Prayer, whether personal, Eucharistic, or group, has one thing in common. It is an effort to enter the space and time of God. Insofar as prayer is successful, space and time can occasionally all but disappear. Physics is one thing, and theology is another, but prayer can conjoin us with "the beyond within." Graced prayer makes communion with God possible and beliefs believable and the future present—and all of these more or less.

What we now know about space-time invites a different imaginary about the afterlife. We can imagine the afterlife in light of the curvature of space-time and therefore as taking place within the boundaries of nature. What adds cogency to this imagining for Christians is the belief and experience that to be in Christ is to be already in the new creation. In Him the "there" is already here, and "then" is now. If the new physics sprouts a theological dimension as recommended here, physics and faith should be able to "see" more, though still only through a glass darkly.

Several "practical" benefits could come from the conversion recommended here. One is that it would be hugely beneficial to nature if the human denizens who live within it could see themselves in communion with it and its Creator rather than merely users of it on their way to some other locale. A second

benefit would be humility. The more we learn about things like
how infinitesimal our planet is vis-à-vis the rest of the universe
and how recent an entry we humans are in the lists of living
things, the more human hubris becomes ridiculous. A third
benefit would be a clearer focus on taking responsibility for
our consciousness and what we store in it and stoke it with.
A fourth benefit would be a continuing acceptance of the
inevitable ignorance we have about afterlife. "The dark night
of the soul" described by the mystics mirrors the mystery of
dark matter that physics has run up against in the universe.
Physicists and mystics have to deal with a similar temptation,
namely whether the quest has been pointless or the dark that's
been encountered in both cases enables observers to slow down
until the "object" speaks more clearly for itself, if and when it
chooses to. The final benefit would be an openness in theology
to a conversion to nature and physics as well as an openness
of scientists, physicists included, to theology.

July 20

I have been thinking about the belief in the soul and its immortality. It was a lot easier to imagine the afterlife as long as the
idea of soul held a place in the self-understanding of believers.
Soul was understood to be the immortal part of a person; it
perdured. It had salvation as its future, and earth was not its
natural home. The mission of the Church was "the salvation
of souls." But once matter and energy operating in space-time
began to intrude on this foundational worldview of soul,
it began to lose its hold on the imagination of the believer.
So where is soul and, even more pointedly, its home beyond
nature—i.e., heaven—now?

I don't claim to know more about the afterlife as a result
of learning about space-time than I did when we had imagined

space and time as separate. What I do know is that we now
have to revisit the projection of a heaven up there and of God
out there and so on because we can now see how our simpler,
ignorant ideas about space and time had space going as far as
it can in extension and time as far as it can in duration with
neither one touching the other. So it was easier to see how
each of these imaginings developed, one into a beyond that is a
place (heaven), the other into a time that is unending (eternity).
One value of the new physics is an awareness that our sensory
perceptions have made these infinities easier to concoct.

∞

July 22   *Resurrection*

The vaunts of some scientists have begun to believe we will be
able to transform ourselves so as to exit our limitations and
transhumanize ourselves through science and technology. This
makes one revisit the hopes one has always entertained about
afterlife. Is that afterlife hope a fantasy? Should I cashier in part
because human intelligence is succeeding in more and more
ways to gain control over our mortality? Some transhumanists
believe that technology will eventually do what religion has
been relied on to do. What further light might the physics of
space-time now provide about the where and when of afterlife?

Since each of us is concerned about staving off our mortality
and death, we all have "skin in the game" of afterlife. The new
physics makes us revisit our erstwhile ideas about the whither
and where of an afterlife and our hopes for it.

Three routes for reflection are available to us. One is reason.
Two is reason open to information. The third is the effort to
align reason and information with faith. This third route is
what has engaged theology throughout the ages. Having learned
what science has found out about space and time, we now
have to see how its findings can be aligned theologically with

Christian hopes about the afterlife. One of course could ignore
the new information (now a hundred years old) and simply be
an evangelist with traditional Christian afterlife hopes.

With creation, space-time came to be. In the new creation
time and space, like everything else, will still be, but transformed, in the direction of a greater communion between God
and nature and one another. Why? Because for those who love
God "all things" work together unto good (Rom. 8:28). In the
case of space-time this would mean that the characteristics of
duration and extension each of which vector out into unintelligibility in the present creation will lose their negatives in the
new creation. The further the distance, the more impossible
communion is, and the longer something goes, the more it will
decay. But these cosmic structures will be transformed. The
transcendent God will become "all in all." Emmanuel, God-
with-us, will move from being a desire and yearning—may
God be with us—to being omnipresent.

Do space-time structures undergo transformation now?
One answer might be found in one's experience, hopefully
and more particularly, through one's prayer experience, especially in Eucharist. Prayer should help one realize that the new
creation is not a wholly future thing but a presence experienced
in moments in the present howsoever dimly or momentarily.

Another source of information about how space-time
structures will change can be found in the resurrection appearances. In these appearances of Jesus we have hints about how
space-time will differ in the new creation. He "appeared" sans
having to travel to get from here to there. The resurrection
appearances take place in space-time without the weight of
distance or duration as these are experienced in the present
creation. It is evident to the witnesses, that he is who he was,
that he has the same "mass and energy," although these are not
terms they would have thought in. I like the way C. S. Lewis in
his *Miracles* (Fontana Books, 1967) imagined the continuity/

discontinuity between the former and the new creation in terms of difference between a waterfall before and after, that is, the same stuff but very changed.

In the resurrection appearances one can imagine what the disciples experienced. To their enormous relief, he is the same person with whom they had been in relationship. Eventually they would be able to believe that what began even before history as relationality between the Father, Son, and Spirit will end in a relational eschaton. And he will be the link the Spirit will be able to make that will get the Christian faith to make this connection.

It is easier to have his hopes and think his way if one expects physics to be able to satisfactorily answer questions that are metaphysical. But even within the findings of physics, things get more inexplicable, not less. For example, the recent and undeniable evidence that the known universe is expanding, and is doing so more and more rapidly. Or that within our own galaxy there are 40 billion "habitable earths."

July 24

Augustine's belief was that our knowledge of God increases if our knowledge of nature increases. And since the natural sciences are learning more and more about nature, we have the opportunity of knowing more about nature's Author. Take, for example, the new evidence about life on earth and its emergence from chemical reactions that brewed between the stars. "Not so long ago, deep space seemed static and dull; now it looks like the possible breeding ground for a blue-print of life that might be shared across all the universe." So it seems now that molecular life began in outer space, although it is not yet clear how it got to our planet. Either way, "life doesn't care about the 'Made in . . .' label on the molecules" (Andrew

Grant, "Cosmic Blue-Print of Life," *Discover,* November 2010, 44). So where does this new knowledge of nature leave us? If true, it seems to me that it would leave us thinking that there is more and more interconnectedness between what God has made and that nothing is superfluous. It doesn't seem that God ever discards anything and that all is part of God's plans. Therefore, "lowly" should be used much less by us the more we know about how beholden we have been and still are to the things of nature.

July 26

Before physics and Einstein came along time was in effect duration. If one were a believer, one lived in hopes of an eternity which would begin after time. So time would cease with the person's entry into eternity. One would live in a new condition, an eternal one, once one expired. Time, too, expired for the dead. What happens to this picture when time and space are combined and lose their character as we had imagined them? I think we can(we)know more about afterlife if we know more about space-time! What is it that we will know?

From theology we know that eternity, eternal life, begins within time not after time, and that the kingdom is not to come but can be experienced as a here-and-now kind of thing. Therefore, we believe that the conditions of heaven are to begin, not when we enter a space other than here, which has been called heaven, but that whatever it is is to be happening in this present space. We also know enough about the incarnation to realize that it was God's commitment to space and time. Jesus' continuing humanity after his death and bodily resurrection is still our best indication of this. His ascension was not an exodus from space and time but an invitation to cling to him and to embrace the whole mystery of him in all its height and depth, length and breadth, including time and space as our knowledge of these expands.

July 29

Lonergan's *On the Way to Nicea* (Westminster Press, 1976), like his larger tome *Insight*, is intellectually challenging. In the book, he runs through cognitive theory, the hermeneutics of the heretics, and the movement from symbol to knowledge that qualifies as critical realism. But he never loses sight of the fact that notwithstanding all the variations in the ideas extant at the time, eventually the dogma of the consubstantiality of Jesus and the Father and the Spirit emerges.

It is remarkable how this particular dogma came from so much variation in the ideas about who Jesus was in relation to God. Lonergan's starting point was that "the word" of Scripture is "true." He then watches the interaction between human intelligence and the Third Person of the Trinity. The result was, as Jesus had promised, truth about who God was and his relation to God.

From within a milieu of wrong judgments, misjudgments, ideology, and factionalism, right judgment emerged. How it did is what makes Lonergan's analysis so valuable. His cognitional theory helps judge where and how the Spirit might be accompanying us and where we might err by going beyond the evidence, or by being inattentive, or irresponsible by a wrong judgment.

Lonergan's cognitional theory enables one to sort out all the oversights and mistaken understandings about Jesus that were circulating before the council to see how the truth of the dogma of Nicea was achieved. The treasure of Lonergan's cognitional theory is the insight it gives into epistemology or, if you will, its implicit epistemological pneumatology. Although

Lonergan understood understanding as few have, it seems to me that we must further his theory by seeing how the Spirit accompanies the whole process.

The scriptural word that is available to all was not enough to stop the differentiations of consciousness that happened in the years after the New Testament was written. These differentiations of consciousness could have torn the Church into pieces had there not been some kind of an authority that could judge them as accurate or inaccurate, as off the mark or on it. One thing that amused and engaged Lonergan was how the slivers of this dogma emerged without many of the contributors realizing that this is what they were building up to. So while subjectivity was being informed about the truth of the identity of Jesus, both Spirit and knowing how right knowing gets done, each helps to explain the authoritative resolution of long inquiry.

Nicea is a perfect case of communal discernment. The exercise of it at Nicea saved the unity of the Church, such as it was at that time. There had to be a right judgment about Jesus' relationship to God. Both unity and truth are helped by greater clarity about method. Both are jeopardized by those who believe they have already been achieved. Truth is an ongoing achievement needing all the help it can get both from the Spirit and from good judgment about how judgments are made well.

An irony in all of this was that every heretic was an occasion for the emergence of the dogma. The more heretics, the more urgent the need became for the right judgments to arrive at an authoritative dogma. It's easy to subscribe to untruth about God not seeing that it is untrue. It's just that intelligence alone isn't as infallible as it would like to be. And infallibility disengaged from intelligence can be not credible. Verifiability about cherished insights is a necessary moment in the move from subjectivity to objectivity. Personal insight has to get legs outside of the person. In other words, discernment is a social activity, not just a personal one.

Can God get bored? This is a very anthropomorphic way of putting it, but I ask it because so many of our subjectivities seem to be stuck in yesterday, and this would bore God, I presume. Why? Because subjectivity, like the Spirit that accompanies it, is naturally creative. Granted, subjectivity can be too creative. It can disregard or even forget its own history. Or it can have such a high regard for yesterday that it can develop an incapacity for being open to the challenges of tomorrow.

Whatever one thinks of the ancient church, Nicea and the other councils did play the referee; otherwise the game would have gotten out of control. Although the striped shirts can drive one crazy, the game with no referees can become hopelessly confused.

This brings us back to method and how it helps in extricating the products of creative subjectivity and judging them. Yesterday's right judgments serve as one measure but not the only one since knowledge necessarily evolves. What was rightly judged yesterday sometimes needs to be reweighed, given today's experience and enlightened by new understandings leading to a further right judgment. In brief, I am thinking of the need for an epistemology for our spiritualities or, better, that a spirituality of epistemology has still to be developed!

August 1

How reliable is God? Does God make covenants and withdraw them after a while if God's initiative is disobeyed? Was the reason why the "old" covenant became the new covenant because Israel didn't respond to God's covenant initiatives? Does the new covenant annul the old one? I don't believe so.

In many ways the same old thing has been going on with all of these divine initiatives. They can all deepen an understanding of God as consistent and reliable and passionate throughout the passage of time—was yesterday, is today, and will be the same forever. No divinely initiated covenant has ever been revoked, annulled, or retracted by God. This same covenanting dynamism took on many forms over the course of Israel's history. We would have considerably more knowledge of God if we let the fact of covenanting as the way God acts have more of a say than we do by pondering the mystery abstracted from covenant. This is also a recommendation for being more historical and empirical than metaphysical and theological.

It is important to notice how during the Old Testament's evolution, Israel's understanding of covenant moves from externals to being more interior and personal and inter-divine/human. To expatiate: the Sinai covenant was written on stone tablets. The new covenant was written on the heart. The old covenant required charismatic leaders and prophets to teach and exhort the people how to live according to the stipulations that were elaborated. In the new covenant the promise is that Yahweh's servant will teach each person in their hearts how they are to understand what they need to know about God, and therefore do and be Godly. The new covenant, furthermore, will not be insular but a light to the nations. Before this interiority and universality take place, covenant became something Yahweh established with David and his household. The Divine Partner in this covenant promises that if the embrace is yielded to, the result will be an eternal dynasty.

What was the role of the Spirit in this evolving understanding of covenant? The Spirit has always made covenant experientially available to human beings, though the Jewish experience was not an awareness of Spirit as such, but of a numinous reality that transcended here and now. The Spirit has always accompanied the operations of consciousness in order to produce knowledge and choices. It does so by serving them, not determining them.

Humans evolve in their understanding of reality and have slowly, slowly developed an understanding of understanding itself. Earlier generations needed instructors to come to a greater sophistication, but little by little, people could find their own reflective capacities and come to personal judgments. The Spirit's accompaniment always deepened the human capacity for interiority.

What was always being sought and attained was transcendent knowledge, knowledge that transcends the subject. What is interesting is that this kind of knowledge was there from the beginning of human consciousness. Our archaeological data finds so much awareness of the transcendently real that was named in so many different ways "God." Again I want to draw attention to John Paul's observation that: "The Spirit's presence and activity are universal, limited by neither space nor time" (*Redemptoris Missio* #28). He goes on to mention Vatican II and its conviction that "the Spirit is at work in the heart of every person, through the seeds of the word, to be found in human initiatives—including religious ones—and in mankind's efforts to attain truth, goodness and God himself." (His references point back to three references in the Council's *Ad Gentes* and six in *Gaudium et Spes*.)

☙

August 3

The most important characteristic of good teaching is that it animates students to want to know what they don't know or even to contribute to what is not yet known by us. Questions that start someone's engines and keep them rolling for potential answers. We want to figure out what hasn't been figured out yet, at least by us. There is a book by Stuart Firestein called *Ignorance* (Oxford University Press, 2012). Both the title and the subject are ingenious. I wonder why it has taken so long and so many books before this one came along.

The author's point is that we should not connect ignorance with being stupid but with desiring to come to new knowledge.

We are aggregators and always in the process of putting together the disaggregated, and getting from the "not yet" to the "already." It is questions that animate the questing self. Thinking, choosing, discerning—these are the acts that bring us into our deeper selves. Firestein, who is a neuroscientist at Columbia University, obviously doesn't value ignorance in itself, just the ignorance that wants to get beyond itself. When he invites other professors to come to talk to his students, he recommends that they talk about what they would like to find out about and why and how they are trying to answer their own questions.

To take just one example of the value of my own ignorance, owned, and overcome. It comes from what I have been learning about the difference between the growth of sea ice in Antarctica and the parallel loss of it in the Arctic. In the winter the sea ice around Antarctica has expanded at one point at 22 square miles a minute, according to satellite reports from 2011. Contrast this to the Arctic where last summer the sea ice was the smallest amount ever recorded since these satellites started tracking this data 33 years ago. The Arctic Ocean is circumscribed by land, North America, Greenland, and Eurasia. By contrast, Antarctica is its own land/sea/ice mass.

For the first time a new factor has been found to explain the difference between the condition of ice in these two polar regions. Wind! Of all things! Some wind blows the ice up on to the shores and piles it up higher and higher on itself. Other wind blows ice floes further and further apart, and the freezing water between them becomes ice. So the wind is driving the ice in two different directions in these two polar regions. Antarctica's sea ice has been expanding every year, and the Arctic ice has been shrinking. Our ignorance still is considerable about how these two poles and their different wind patterns affect the rest of the planet's climate. But for the first time in history, wind seems to be the new known that affects every place and person on the planet (see Robert Lee Hotz, *Wall Street Journal*, November 12, 2012).

I am bemused by this new knowledge about wind and, at the same time, our ignorance about it. I recall Nicodemus wondering how a man can be born again after he has already been born. Jesus answered Nicodemus's question in wind terms: "The wind blows where it will. You hear the sound it makes but you do not know where it comes from or where it goes. So it is with everyone begotten of the Spirit" (John 3:8). In the Greek, *pneuma* can mean wind or spirit.

Now this is interesting! While wind might become key to our understanding of weather, we now have new knowledge about our ignorance of it. The same thing is true about the wind that is the Spirit! There are parallels here. Increasingly, we have knowledge, and knowledge of our ignorance about weather-wind and divine Wind. Now that we know more and more about the contrasting effects of wind on both Poles we know there is so much more we need to know about it. The same is true about the effects of the Spirit's presence or absence.

For those who do not experience faith as a source of knowledge, comparing these two kinds of wind might sound like apples and oranges, a vacuous exercise in neither here nor there. For some, the empirical is the only source of knowledge that is of any value. But that does not seem true even for them, because even empiricists have enough faith in their thinking to believe in their empiricism. To undertake the action of cognition that entails the belief that it is worthwhile. Both the burden and value of being human is that we are able to value and weigh and act on what we learn. Like it or not, we all have faith, at least that grasping reality and evaluating what we judge to be so is essential. One's faith might be worldly or obscure or secular, but it is still faith. To be able to keep going, we believe knowing is necessary.

But for those who believe that the Wind can unfurl sails that otherwise stay dead in the water, it's a different story. St. Paul calls the effects of the Spirit, "fruits." There are two different metaphors at hand to try to have some understanding of the Spirit, one that likens it to fruit growing in the soil of humans, the other that likens it to sails blown in the direction of the good and true and beautiful. You can harvest fruit—where would we be if we hadn't? And you can harness wind power—what if our ancestors hadn't learned that? We should believe this wind has only begun to make its power manifest. The Spirit has always blown humans into making connections. The fruits of the Spirit are in the direction of solidarity.

The presence of Spirit, according to Paul, has the effect of "joy, peace, patient endurance, kindness, generosity, faith, mildness, chastity" (Gal. 5:22–23). The absence of Spirit and the effect is likely to be: "lewd conduct, impurity, licentiousness, idolatry, sorcery, hostilities, bickering, jealousy, rage, rivalry, dissensions, factions" (vv. 19–20).

August 5

Christians inherited knowledge of the Spirit from Jewish believers who had experienced that presence time and time again. The Spirit that "descended upon him in bodily form like a dove" after Jesus' baptism was not making its debut on earth at the river Jordan (Luke 3:22). Granted, It was not considered a Divine Person by Jews nor was Its relation to God understood. But Its presence, often referred to as "Shekhinah" (a holy radiance), was amply testified to in Judaism.

What the connection was and is between God and Shekhinah is a subject that has crossed many a rabbi's eyes. This feminine Hebrew word conveyed experiences of God's tangible presence, especially in the Temple in Jerusalem. The Spirit caused the experience of the numinous, but more enduringly, prophecies. It was imagined by Isaiah as the train of the Lord's robes filling the Temple (e.g., Isa. 6:1). All of which is to say, there was an expectation and an experience of God being able to be tangibly present to the People of Israel. The Talmud claims that the Shekhinah is present in a special way when three judges are gathered to discern, or when ten are at prayer or at the side of a sick person.

One of the awakenings in the twentieth century for Christians was the realization that the greatest disaster visited upon Jews, namely the Holocaust, was linked to the history of Christian denigration of Jews. One of the sources of this cruel hubris was that they had parochialized the Spirit by believing that they had something special that Jews didn't have. The Holocaust should have been a wake-up call to Christians about antisemitism just as climate change should be today about our inveterate anthropocentrism. Nature is the medium that is sending this latter message loud and clear. Unhappily, the deaths of 6 million Jews is the undeniable historical record of one erroneous worldview. Ecology conveys the needed evidence of another erroneous worldview.

There are four right judgments that could generate repentance and healing and right relationships with Jews. First of all, that God is faithful and that God committed the God self (little did they know—it was Father, Son, and Spirit) irrevocably to a people in the covenants that Israel was invited into. Jeremiah names this irrevocability by saying that the sun, moon, and stars, and the sea and its tides, will vanish sooner than will "the offspring of Israel . . . cease from being a nation before Me forever" (Jer. 31:36). God has never revoked the covenant that was made to "my people, Israel."

Second, that the human proclivity to have an identity, especially a religious identity, that is acquired by the righteous construing a god who sees the other as unrighteous is not of God. God's choice of *us* does not make a *them*. There is no *them* to God.

Third, that one cannot hope to write or read a biography of the Spirit by ignoring the work of the Spirit before the work of the Spirit that Jesus was. The Spirit was responsible for the incomparably high artistry of numerous previous embodiments. The people who followed Jesus were in a continuum with the processions of the people from whom he came and through and with whom he grew in wisdom, age, and grace. Jesus' Jewishness was not anomalous, nor was his concinnity to the Wind.

Fourth, we have to repot the Spirit story, transplanting it from the smaller pot Christian history has put it in to a much larger one. Some theologians who have tried to do this have suggested changing the name to "the Spirit of the God of Israel" rather than "the Spirit of Christ." Geoffrey Lampe (e.g., his *God as Spirit* [London: SCM Press, 1977]) has stressed the need to "lay great emphasis on the continuity of God's creative work in the process of cosmic evolution, in the development of man, and especially in the continuing creation and salvation of human beings" (96).

In the Hebrew scriptures, there is a discernible movement from spirit/Spirit as wind/breath of God (ruach) to the prophetic word of God (davar), to the wisdom of God (Sophia) to God as accessible through inspired texts. This movement—from ruach to davar to Sophia—was susceptible of being categorized and thereby of domesticating the Spirit. In general, it has been difficult to leave the Spirit free without subordinating it to the identity needs of a group or a moment or a person, even the Person of Jesus.

August 8

Although one can believe that the Spirit is the Lord and Giver of Life, still one's empirical mind needs to know how this happens. A remarkable contribution to answering such a question is a major study that has been undertaken by the Human Microbiome Project. It is a consortium of more than two hundred scientists from eighty institutions which has been organized by the National Institutes of Health to sequence the material of bacteria taken from a carefully preselected number of 250 healthy people. The findings are stunning even though the conclusions from this information are still only developing. This project found that 100 trillion microbes are alive in each of us. In some ways they function like we are their home. In fact, one researcher would go so far as to wonder whether each of us is "an assemblage of life forms living together." This project should prompt anthropological puzzlements. The Stanford microbiologist David Rieman comments that insofar as we are microbial, we are very similar to coral.

A recent piece by Matt Ridley in his Mind and Matter column titled "Bug Me" (*Wall Street Journal,* July 1, 2012) playfully reminds readers of some things from this study—for example, the fact that each of us resembles "a zoo of microbes"; that each of us is 90 percent bacterial cells by bodily weight, even though the little critters are so infinitesimal; that there are ten times more bacterial cells in a healthy gut than there are in the rest of one's entire body. Remember that these "things" are not just passengers; they are colleagues necessary for digestion and for fighting infection, etc. They co-evolve with us.

Humans have been presuming for a very long time that each of us has a personal identity or is a distinctly different instance of *Homo sapiens.* The findings of this microbiome project would affirm that, as each person's collection of microbes is unique. But at the same time the sheer multiplicity of them in each person makes it clear that we have to go back to the drawing board and ask, given the microbial flotsam-jetsam we now know is operating in all of us, what is a personal identity? This is not a question the Microbiome Project asked itself. Nor is it likely to, since its interest is about health, more accurately about how to use the information being amassed about bacteria to have good bacteria keep bad bacteria at bay.

This new information about bacteria flies in the face of the bad reputation bacteria have had ever since it was known there were bacteria. In fact two new industries have developed in the twentieth century from this knowledge: antibiotics and probiotics. One of the more intriguing facts about antibiotics is that 80 percent of the antibiotics produced in the United States are consumed by the animals we in turn consume. They are fed these not to fight bad bacteria but to have them grow larger so that there is more of them for us to eat.

Besides an antibiotics industry, there is also a probiotics industry developing as a result of our growing knowledge of bacteria. It is enjoying increasing success. To cite a specific example: this new industry has learned that good bacteria from the stool of a healthy person can be extracted and fashioned into a suppository for an infected patient to improve the latter's bacterial ecosystem. There is a growing success being reported about this process.

One of the sites the scientists of this project examined for bacteria was the vagina. They found that the bacteria in the vaginal tract changes significantly in the first trimester of pregnancy. The bacteria that were there in abundance before pregnancy become rare while what was rare before becomes abundant. One of these new bacteria is called *Lactobacillus johnsonii*. During delivery these bacteria will swathe the baby as it passes through the birth canal, and the effect of these in the infant enables it subsequently to digest its mother's breast milk. In addition, the mother's milk has been found to contain 600 species of bacteria, most of it of the good variety. Through nursing, these bacteria are how the ordinary infant's microbiome develops.

This Microbiome NIH project has been undertaken so that science can see more deeply into the connection between health and bacteria. The microbiome holds more of an answer to the how of life than any previous age could have imagined. The scientists took their data from particular bacterial sites in the bodies of their subjects. What they found were disease-causing bacteria in every microbiome, but, alas, these were living peacefully among the overwhelming number of good ones. One would have to wonder, if each of us is really a carrier of 100 trillion microbes, what is a me, who is a me, how do these get packaged in the one me? Do they carry us, or we them? The challenge we have is to try to appropriate this tsunami of biological information into these anthropological questions.

I have a candidate for trying to figure out how these 100 trillion bacteria can each have their own character while I function as ignorant of them as they of me. The many are somehow one. My candidate doesn't come from data uncovered by science, though it claims to be no less in the real world than bacteria. For someone who doesn't think God is part of the real world, this kind of thinking will be dismissed.

My candidate is God, more particularly, the character of God as many yet one. The Christian way of remaining mono-theist evolved into believing God's reality is actually Trinitarian. I think this might have something to say to the puzzlement about how each of us carries such a complex multiplicity while experiencing ourselves as one. If this is how God was from the beginning, is now, and ever shall be, might this give us a way of grounding this new, bewildering data about multiplicity in some intelligibility? Starting with God the Creator of every-thing, the communion of the three Divine Persons might be a prototype of the subsequent multiplicity of everything all the way down to the data uncovered by this project?

So the belief that the Spirit is the Giver of Life has now exponentially more complexity about what goes into it than when it was articulated as a belief of the faith of the Church. A bacterium is something living. How about 100 trillion microbes?—they are too. And in any one person each bacterium has its own life and capability. And that capability can be good or bad. We are just scratching the surface of this information and would do well to be puzzled by it. Bacteria and microbes are not the source of our lives but without them we would not be living. How is it that their infinitesimal capacities work in a continuum, ordinarily, with me their host with clearly my own series of purposes? And where were the 75 species of bacteria living now in my mouth living before they ended up in my mouth? The more microbial data that is amassed, the more wonderful it is, and the more explanations and integration we need with it.

How to get any explanations beyond the simply empirical? Empirically we have more and more data without having explanations of the questions it raises. Some kind of method and discipline that is transempirical is needed to satisfy one's questions beyond the scientific. A transcendental method seeks answers with intelligence as the engine. But the use of intelligence has any number of traditions that it has access to, which have proved satisfying to those who have subscribed to or contributed to them. Theology is one of these. Pneumatology is one branch of Christian theology that has been interested in life questions, its beginnings, its destiny, and what living because of the Spirit might entail by way of belief and behavior. How does the Spirit relate to, or direct, or assist my personal microbiome?

Experience is the first operation of consciousness that needs to be examined about this question. The need, for example, to take care of yourself is pretty general and gets very specific when you know you haven't or when you need something to get you from illness back to health. The second operation of consciousness is understanding. I can recall or learn from or seek advice from any number of ways of understanding what I need to know, like when I experience a particular illness.

Insight into the cause of an illness and the means of getting well produces judgment and action. Transcendental methodology gets more from subjectivity to objectivity. But the operation of understanding is where multiple bodies of knowledge can enter the picture as the person tries to make sense of one's selfhood. Come to think of it, the incarnation was an instance of a new microbiome. It might be repugnant to put it this way but Jesus of Nazareth was an ecosystem of bacteria on two legs. This doesn't exhaustively describe him, obviously, but if I am and you are, he was and is. If there isn't a fit here, then he wasn't one of us. But he was and still is, so there is a fit.

August 11

Geology is only about two centuries old as a science. It has been uncovering the secrets Mother Earth has been hiding for these many millennia. I want to focus on just one little bit of earth's recently uncovered secrets: graptolites. Their history is interred in earth's bones, that is, in stone and rock.

Graptolites thrived some 500 million years ago. They were living organisms. They were literally innumerable so that trying to imagine their number would be an exercise in futility. They have been traced by stratigraphers, that smallish group of geologists who specialize in examining what rock strata can disclose. It is in strata of rock that these minute organisms still attest to their quondam existence.

Even though these stones can't cry out, we can. Even though they are silent, we don't have to be silent about them. Though they are now embedded as a timeless witness, they can be an occasion for us to "rejoice and praise God" for the life they once had and that we now enjoy (Luke 20:37–40).

There are three things that are particularly intriguing about these graptolites (the name is from two Greek words that mean

literally written and rock). One is that each of them is unique.
Two is their sociality. Three is their extinction.

I came to appreciate how unique each graptolite was from
an article in the *New Yorker* (December 23, 2013), "The Lost
World," by Elizabeth Kolbert, who writes on scientific matters.
On an expedition with some stratigraphers she found one of
these fossils in the shape of a feather, another like a fern's frond,
another lyre-like. And would you believe it, she even found one
that resembled a set of false eyelashes.

What is interesting about this is that their distinctiveness
and sameness are folded in together. Like snowflakes, come to
think of it. Like us—all different, but all of the same nature.
This is also redolent of the Trinity. Three Persons, each distinct
but at the same time having the same nature, the only instance
of the essence of divinity that has ever been, is now, and ever
will be. It's as if one of the Three has the false eyelashes, the
Other . . .

Even though the only remaining evidence we have of them
is preserved in rock, these marine animals were swimmers back
in their day. But not lone swimmers, interestingly enough. The
rocks give evidence of their being in colonies. Though each one
had built around itself a tube-like shelter known as a theca, it
was attached to other graptolites like row houses are attached
to one another.

What comes to mind with this geological factoid is another
archaeological site being dug up from first-century Nazareth.
Although the Christian imagination has had the Holy Family
in some singular dwelling, sniffing incense so to speak, apart
from the lowing herd, the evidence now is that Jesus, Mary,
and Joseph lived enmeshed with other families in hutches
dependent on a communal fireplace. Whatever the singularity
that emerged from this arrangement, the communality of a
village was what nurtured it. Maybe Mary and Joseph leaving
Jesus in the Temple for three days is a good way of seeing

how interdependent Nazarene families were on one another. In general, fact-fed faith repots revelation, de-leafing some of its preternaturalness.

The third thing that intrigues me is both the life of these little graptolites and the catastrophe that laid them waste. As far as I know, they came to be the same way so many other organisms came to be, that is, from the deep water hydro-vents that spewed forth all the chemical and biochemical ingredients that have generated so many species on this planet. They flourished by the billions in the Paleozoic era half a billion years ago. Though "how" they lived gets some clarity from the aforesaid data, "why" they came to be only God knows. But a few things can be said about why. God is love and gives life because of love, even to such tiny little and numerous animals as these. Living things are alive because of God's love. Where life is, God's love is why they are.

What lives, though, is mortal. Only God is eternal. Some living things have stories to tell about themselves and about other living things—about life and mortality. One of these accounts of meaning claims to have its authorship from God and developed beliefs like those mentioned in the previous paragraphs.

About graptolites and their extinction. Apparently it was swift, sudden, final. The cause: glaciation! Glaciers coming up from the Southern Hemisphere even before continents such as Australia and Africa had formed. If God is love, why would love create living things that end up dying? This is where one of the stories humans tell themselves about life gets interesting. It is a story about living after dying and participating in the eternity of God because of the love that had created them and the rest of stuff that had come to life in the first place. It remains for the storytellers to try to make the connections between the graptolites' life and death and Jesus' life and death, and everything that has life but is mortal.

August 14

In religious language, several conversions are needed; in more earthy language, we need two repottings. The first one entails extricating the image of the self and our species and rooting it more clearly in the soil of earth or within the materiality of the planet and the physical universe. The second repotting entails taking the faith-in-God story, having relocated it in its natural home, nature, and put it together with more recent data about the beginnings of *Homo sapiens*.

These two repottings would make wholes where dichotomies have been erroneously construed for far too long. These conversions are urgently needed for the earth's well-being, on the one hand, and the faith's reliability, on the other. For too long we have clothed ourselves as a species vis-à-vis the other species in false understandings, thereby disarranging the natural order of things. Anthropocentrism is a mistake about human identity. It has been reinforced by anthropologies that made humans see themselves as other than the rest of what's in the garden. We have the responsibility to come to right judgment, beginning with ourselves. Wrong judgment both about ourselves and the garden produces a poor crop and eventually will result in no crop and no successor gardeners.

So how do we go about this needed repotting? By trying to align the sacred texts with the scientific data. For starters, the data of paleoanthropology with the Christology of Philippians. "Christ Jesus, who, though he was in the form of God, did not regard equality with God as something to be exploited, but emptied himself, taking the form of a slave; being born in human likeness, and being found in human form, he humbled himself and became obedient to the point of death" (Phil. 2:5–8). Having initially been "in the form of God" his divine consciousness would have known what we human beings are only now learning about the tattered emergent origins of the humanity he emptied himself into. Another example, the genealogy in Matthew 1:1–17 that begins with Abraham has to be informed by the emerging evidence coming from paleoanthropology and our way-back-then ancestry. Now for some of the data from paleoanthropology: In 2010 the Max Planck Institute for Evolutionary Anthropology in Germany announced finding Neanderthal DNA in the genome of modern Europeans. So much for Adam and Eve, or at least as we have imagined such a proto pair. But the evidence gets even more complex. In an issue of the journal *Cell*, published July 25, 2012, there is evidence of what is now called "a sister species" to Neanderthals and, therefore, one that is in a kinship with us humans. This data comes from Africa and date back between 20 to 50 thousand years ago, even before Neantherthals migrated to Europe and mated with humans. So apparently not only do we have Neanderthal genes in our gene pool, but also something of their African siblings.

Another piece of evidence to throw into this muddle of our early origins is a species called the Denisovans. This is evidence found in Siberia, of all places, and in the Pacific Islands where the DNA of a people calls into question whether *Homo sapiens* is a unique species or a mélange of species. The evidence is increasingly coming to the second conclusion.

A book by the British paleoanthropologist Chris Stringer imaginatively titled *Lone Survivors: How We Came to Be the Only Humans on Earth* (Times Books, 2012) has consolidated much of this recent material about human origins. Some of the factoids: modern humans (us) have about 2.5 percent of Neanderthal DNA in them. So it is certain there was interbreeding. It is also likely that these copulations took place in caves in the general region of present-day Israel, Syria, and Lebanon, since there were Neanderthals and humans living in those regions at the same time. The surmise is that the interbreeding was infrequent but enough to leave unmistakable genetic traces. The information is still developing. For example, in 1987 there was a relative consensus about a hypothesis that there was an Eve and that she was African and that she was around 200 thousand years ago. She had a daunting adjective describing her, "Mitochondrial"—the Mitochondrial Eve. But this hypothesis has now been seen as too simple because of evidence gathered since then. Stringer wrote, "If we went back 100,000 years which is very recent, geologically speaking, there might have been as many as six different kinds of humans on earth. . . . We are the lone survivors" (*New York Times,* July 17, 2012).

August 20

To repeat myself, it would be wonderful to read an autobiography of the Holy Spirit, one written by the author "Himself." (Or Itself?) The uncertainty of the pronoun only adds to the need for such a tome. But it would be a prodigious feat, both writing it and reading it. How to satisfy the desire for such a product? Obviously, at best one would have to settle for a biography. But who would be the author, in this case? Or the co-author? Mother Nature, I believe, is continuing to play such a role. The only problem is her style. She seems to shred what she writes, so one has to piece it together one sliver at a time. And juxtaposing the slivers together until a face begins to appear is not an assured undertaking, especially for the impatient. Though the face promises to be holy and awesome, its visibility also requires some input from the would-be reader—like faith, hope, love—all three, buckets-full.

Let me take one of the shreds available to all of us, the event of Hurricane Sandy. It churned up the east coast of the Atlantic for some days, having wreaked havoc in a number of places including Jamaica and Haiti before it hit landfall north of Cape May, New Jersey. From there it continued its voracious and punitive path for some 900 miles west and north.

The first thing to notice about this shred of this would-be biography is that it seems to have a large agenda, and humans seem to be only part of it. It's not all about us. To employ an awkward term, the lens of anthropomorphism doesn't make reading or writing this biography easy. But nature is either the Spirit's tool or the Spirit befriends it. In the course of trying to read this sliver of the biography of Spirit, climatologists have two things to say about events like Sandy. One is that humans are part of the cause of the problem. The other is that in the long run this kind of event is a source of planetary health, hence good for creatures on the planet, which includes us who are humans. That is hard to believe, of course, for those who have been caught in its destruction.

For those who don't believe there is a Spirit or don't believe that if there is that it is connected to nature, it is just a hurricane. "So, hold off on the biography, theology, pneumatology, etc." There is therefore a choice. Either to believe or not to believe. I choose to believe that there is both nature and more, and the Spirit has more to say than Sandy said.

Granted we were taught the story about God by our faithful predecessors who had the advantage of cosmological innocence. In more recent centuries we have been losing some of that innocence. We began by congratulating ourselves about our knowledge of the Milky Way. But now we learn that it is only one in a cosmos of millions of galactic solar systems. We and planet earth, it turns out, are a microscopic blip in a massive, unimaginably massive universe. So where are we?

We have also been innocents about time. What time is it? Now that we find out that at the center of our own galaxy there is a black hole that devours matter that was the measure by which to tell time, what time is it? A black hole has been called "a matter-eating beast" (Caleb Scharf, *Gravity's Engines: How*

Bubble-Blowing Black Holes Rule Galaxies, Stars, and Life in the Cosmos [Farrar, Straus and Giroux, 2012]).

The cosmological estimation of the time of the universe's birth is around 14 billion years ago.

A further conundrum for a biography of the Spirit is the relation between these black holes and life. It has been central to the Christian story to believe that the Spirit is "the Lord and Giver of Life." How does one understand and tell the story of the Spirit if black holes are the death of the living things they eat? Just to confuse things even more, some of the recent hypotheses of astronomy and cosmology that are winning attention are linking the beginning of life to the activity of black holes! Since they clearly birth stars, and stars are clearly a major source of explanation of life, could it be that the Spirit, the Lord and Giver of Life, has been birthing life through black holes? What a challenge! The paschal mystery that is a key ingredient of course of our faith-story has life coming from death. We have much more to learn about black holes and the expansion of the universe and the value of hurricanes than we presently know. All I know is that the empirical is a good source of answers but a better source of questions.

August 23

To succeed in this effort of doing a biography of the Spirit through nature and our growing knowledge of it, I need to learn to "think like a mountain." This pregnant metaphor comes from Aldo Leopold and his reflection as a mountain ranger working for the US Forest Service in Arizona and New Mexico in the 1920s. Through a number of very vivid scenes he conveys how he has come to understand the difference between rationality, his own and humans' in general, and the rationality he found to be latent in nature. Not nature in some abstract way but the nature he learned about from specific moments. One day he saw "the fierce green fire" in the eyes of the dying old wolf who was shot by a team of which Leopold was a part, more or less "for the hell of it." The riflemen never imagined what "the mountain thought." What Leopold awakened to, as this and other scenes convey, is the destruction by technology of nature, by ignorant reason over the wisdom of a mountain, and by whim over a life. "There was something new to me in those eyes—something known only to me and to the mountain" (*A Sand County Almanac and Sketches Here and There* [Oxford University Press, 1987], 130).

There is much that this metaphor evokes. By trying to think like something wholly other than the way we humans think, the challenge is to *put on* the mind of the other as best we can. In my case the other is not a mountain but a Divine Other. Is that even possible? Not fully, obviously. But in this case the other whose mind one would put on is the One in whose image and likeness I and the rest of our species have been made. So despair at any linkage is unwarranted. Although the mountain's otherness yields only a glimpse into the wisdom it houses, taking on the mind of Christ is more doable and tangible.

To do so is to "take on" the mind of one of us who embodied the Spirit, namely Christ, and who with the Father sent the same Spirit to enable those who receive it, to know both his "mind" (Phil. 2:5) and the Spirit's mind and the Father's mind. They are all "of one mind."

August 26

Notwithstanding our ignorance, humans have been beholden to the Spirit all along. Although the Spirit is free in what It does and how It does it, it seems there is something predictable in Its ordinary way of acting. Some grasp of this should make it

easier to know how the Spirit accompanies us. The surest place
to start is to see the Spirit assisting Jesus in his own developing
understanding of who he was. Since he emptied himself and
became one of us, he experienced everything a child experiences
. . . such as wonder, fright, himself, his parents, his playmates,
his village, his sexuality, nice people, unkindness, the synagogue,
the faith of the people, praying, doubting, thinking. And as he
matured, he learned how to be both self-critical and critical
about what he was thinking and how to do that better. He
was one of the faithful, like his mother and father were. As a
person of faith, he also had a sense of how some versions of
it made more sense than others.

He was both the beneficiary of where evolution had come
from at his moment in time and jeopardized by where it hadn't
yet gone. He was the beneficiary of his culture, both its depth
and its myopia. He learned *modo humano*. If we imagine him
learning in an interventionist mode via divine intervention or
as not needing to learn, that distances his humanity from us
and probably helps distance us from ourselves. One of the
great values of a *modo humano* way of coming to verifiable
insight is it should enable us to understand how the Spirit
accompanies us in our trying to learn and do the truth we
need to learn and do.

Jesus learned "from below," in other words, the way we
learn, even though his self-understanding was free from the
biases that accompany sinfulness. His, therefore, was an understanding that the accompanying Spirit could work with more
easily than with one who has to slog through the myopia of
his or her own selfishness. There can be a greater identifica-
tion with him if we see Jesus developing through experience
attended to attentively, and with understandings weighed
intelligently. His emergent insights and his ways of verifying
them and living faithfully with them and acting with integrity
with his conclusions make him a model of human authenticity.

In other words, an epistemology that notices how consciousness is accompanied by the Spirit will reap the benefits both
religiously and commonsensically.

If anyone was accompanied by the Spirit, Jesus was. His
understandings developed from his own experiences and
from the further understandings he took to them, and from
the insights he arrived at, the skills at judgment he developed,
and his fidelity to these. What is interesting about the early
church's understanding of him and of itself is that it seemed
to develop the same way. The worshipping community had
a unique experience of God that had understanding Jesus at
its center and of the Spirit assisting it in coming to its own
self-understandings. This is what produced the Church and
its beliefs and Gospel texts. Therefore it would be good to
see the similarity between the cognitional processes whereby
he came to understand himself and they came to understand
themselves. This is a methods issue, as well as it is a religious
one. The point is that there is a similarity in the way the Spirit
would accompany intentionality in everyone.

August 28

My reflection today is wrapped around Maria, a friend of
mine. She is a member of a project of which I am a part that
is trying to get scientists to be more interested in theology,
and theologians to be more knowledgeable about science. Her
meticulous work is in immunogenetics. What she is trying to
learn scientifically is in function of the treatment of diseases.
She has to access and assess her data accurately. Her finding
would be dismissed if there were any whiff of anything imported
into her work that was not empirically verifiable.

I will call this side of her her proximacy side in the sense
that the data has to be in material that is being uncovered by

her, hence, proximate. Science is as good as its evidence, and
its evidence emerges from matter. What Maria also brings to
her work is an active faith in God and Christ. I will call this
the ultimacy side of her. Though ultimate can sound remote
in contrast to proximate, this isn't so for her. Her faith is the
milieu in which she lives and moves and has her being.

So she is a scientist who has a tangible religious faith. What
I find fascinating about her is her comfort with both faith and
science. Her very technical research area I can't even name
since it is steeped in all the arcana of her field and its rapid
development. It has something to do with a particular gene
and the promise that more knowledge of it holds for being a
source of healing. But it should be said—and it is said by other
scientists around the table—that the more they discover about
their particular lore, the more daunting their fields become,
since a lifelong sought-for win can result in a stunning loss.
For example a pharmaceutical breakthrough when actually
administered to a patient can sometimes have an adverse effect
because of unpredictables in a given patient.

One of the project participants described it this way: "We
probe into more and more minuscule material and develop a
wonder drug only to find that its use by some people in really
dire situations is not improved but worsened. So we have to
back up out of the narrow and try to see the larger picture
and connect to what others have learned about the bodies we
treat." Part of this upward, wider, larger inquiry generates the
questions the humanities have been dealing with for so long.
There are dimensions of health beyond bodily well-being. There
are healing narratives that come from a past (religious and
philosophical) that can educate science and medicine in tandem.

Maria has a third dimension to her person beyond proximacy and ultimacy. I will call it intimacy. When she describes
being moved by intimacy, she rings true. Not just because of
her marriage, which both she and her husband describe as very

happy, but by intimacy with God as well as with others. She doesn't seem to dichotomize her loving. She breathes intimacy. Sure other things are working, like hormones, her needs, her biases, desire to be loved, etc. But she seems wise about which affections are consonant with God and give evidence of the Spirit. She also seems to be discriminating about whether her affects could be from something else.

Reflecting on what she has shared with us leads me to a further musing. The mission of the Spirit is the well-being of the world, and It pursues it through human denizens, in particular how they go about thinking and choosing. Conversely, the Spirit has a particular interest in this thinking/choosing species not being wrong in their thinking/choosing since being wrong undoes the fabric of the cosmos in some very particular, minute way. So attunement to right thinking and choosing is to God's greater glory.

But this locale of human intentionality where the Spirit is at work is very personal in two senses. One, the Spirit is a Person, and two, Its most delicate work is in persons each of whom is equipped to discern what their better self might be and do in the very particular circumstances. The reverence with which the Spirit works in persons is as self-emptied. Its voice is virtually inaudible, hence seldom noticed or acknowledged. Its work in and with one's better self, therefore, can go unacknowledged for a lifetime. That doesn't say much for one's attention. It may say more about negligences within their education, maybe even more specifically, a poverty in Christian catechesis.

Extrapolating from my experience of Maria, there seems to be something missing if the troika in her—proximacy, ultimacy, and intimacy—is not the expectation and experience of the mature Christian. A solely Christological faith doesn't seem sufficient to take in the concreteness of the mission of the Spirit. This is not to dichotomize Christ from the Spirit but to note that within the distinctiveness of each person's consciousness

the Spirit is uniquely at work, or would be. The more expectation we can bring to this belief and the more able one is at
recognizing this, the more certain the mission of the Spirit will
succeed in that person in their lifetime.

If the mission of the Spirit in human intentionality were
to be given more attention, it seems to me the Marias of this
world would be multiplied exponentially. I wonder too, whether
the brevity of the Apostles' Creed—"we believe in the Holy
Spirit, the Holy catholic church, the communion of saints,
the forgiveness of sins, the resurrection of the body and life
everlasting. Amen"—does justice to the work of the Spirit in
all consciousness.

August 30

So the belief that the Spirit is the Giver of Life is so much more
complex than when it was first articulated. It "gives life" in
the strangest way to the strangest things, like a bacterium or a
microbe. How about 100 trillion! And in each of us each bacterium has its own capability. And that capability can be good or
bad. We are just scratching the surface of this new information
and should be astonished by it. Bacteria and microbes are not
the explanation of our lives, but without them we would not
be living. How is it that their infinitesimal capacities work in
such a continuum, ordinarily, with me who is their host with
my own supervenient purposes? The more microbial data that is
amassed the more questions it raises and explanations it needs.

Empirically we have more and more data without the data
giving any explanation of the questions one can raise about
it. Some kind of transempirical discipline seems needed to
satisfy one's questions, and a method that gets answers with
intelligence as the engine. But intelligence has any number of
traditions that it has access to. They each have a history of

satisfying those who have subscribed to them otherwise they wouldn't continue from generation to generation. Some of these traditions are religious.

One of these religious traditions is Christian, and within Christianity, pneumatology has been particularly interested in life questions, its beginnings, its destiny, and what living in and because of the Spirit could mean. How does the Spirit relate to and assist my own microbiome in its and my or our living together?

What legitimates relating the mystery of the Trinity to this data? Several things: the need to understand the age-old questions like the one and the many, not to mention distinctive personhood itself. Also the absence of anthropological or metaphysical answers that develop from this kind of project. Further, the fact that the Trinitarian understanding of God has been a mainstay for millions of people and still is. And finally, the fact that the microbial data amassed is of a scientific character, and science itself doesn't pursue nonscientific questions and therefore doesn't satisfy those who have them.

But what is even more attractive is the way the Trinity was imagined by the Cappadocians in the fourth century. Their image or insight was called *perichoresis*, the Three as a dance. The early Christians had to develop an understanding of God that remained as monotheistic as their Jewish faith had taught them, and yet they needed to make room for the possibility that this one God always was, is now. and will be forever an interpersonal choreography. Analogously, we are one and many, but so much more multifaceted than we could have ever imagined before microbiology taught us about our personhood as constitutively microbiomic. Although the connection between Divine Personhood and the human person is only analogous, still one can appreciate the continuum between both and come to an understanding about data that otherwise remain just bewildering.

Martin Nowak, the director of the Program for Evolutionary Dynamics at Harvard University, has been writing about the evolution of biological cooperation for the last two decades. His most recent book, *SuperCooperators: Altruism, Evolution and Why We Need Each Other to Succeed,* written with Roger Highfield (Free Press, 2012), is a perfect companion piece to the bacterial data for the microbiome and, in turn, for Trinitarian perichoresis. Each is a case of "super-cooperators."

September 3

This kind of data should leave one awed at the largesse and condescension of the Logos and drama that the Incarnation was just from the point of view of God. It seems that the scene between Jesus and the Samaritan woman is germane here. He tells her "the hour is coming when you will worship the Father neither on this mountain nor in Jerusalem . . . but in Spirit and in truth" (John 4:22–23). The Spirit enables worship and the worshippers to do the connecting of the dots they need to do. Connector is who the Spirit is; connect is what the Spirit does.

There are several ways to think about this connection between these factoids about our earliest forebears and what was in the mind of "the Second Person of the Blessed Trinity" before the event of the incarnation. One is the knowledge of what we are only now coming to know. Hence the humility of what was entailed in his becoming one with "the form of man." Another way to think of it is about love, that God "so loved the world," including these emergents about whom we are learning, including the admixture we have been, that he chose to come into on our side of reality. A third way is to connect the creedal belief that "the Spirit is the Lord and Giver of Life" and that Jesus' incarnation would have entailed an accompaniment of the Spirit into the condition of genus *Homo*. A fourth way is to see the incarnation as an unparalleled opportunity for *Homo sapiens* to understand its connection to the divine genus from which all of this has emerged, is emerging, and will, hopefully, continue to emerge.

The Spirit is the Connector between the old and the new creation. The New Creation will be the real thing, not a presence witnessing to an absence. The ascension was an event connoting the disappearance of a presence followed by a longing for a return. The new creation is the gradual reappearance of that presence, but it is only dimly perceived in the present time.

A relational ontology veers toward connection and continuity rather than disconnection and discontinuity. More empirically, "Carbon atoms are the same particles in graphite and diamond," Wilkinson slyly notes (*Christian Eschatology and the Physical Universe* [T. & T. Clark, 2010], 155). The same might be said of the relation of space-time to matter whether pre- or postresurrection.

September 5

St. Paul was his day's quintessential transhumanist. He named the perennial human desire to "clothe the corruptible body with incorruptibility" or to enfold "mortality with immortality." Today's transhumanism has the same aspiration to have death lose its sting. But its faith is in science and technology, present and to come (1 Cor. 15:55).

Freeman Dyson exemplifies this kind of aspiration. He believes that the combination of human intelligence and the potentiality latent in matter will be able to deliver our hoped-for afterlife. Through genetic engineering biological life can be changed and redesigned so that organisms will even be able to deal with the prospects of a heat death universe (Wilkinson, 18). It would require that human consciousness can be transferred to new kinds of hardware and artificial intelligence over the next trillion years. It is easier to have Dyson's hopes and think his way if one sees human consciousness as a complex physical structure and potentially able to produce its own peculiar kind of immortality. I don't think either of these beliefs is credible.

Frank Tipler is another transhumanist. He connects life with the processing of information and imagines our immortality able to be carried on via computers. He has articulated "The Final Anthropic Principle," which holds that "intelligent information processing must come into existence in the Universe and once it comes into existence it will never die out"(Wilkinson, 19). The Omega Point is where God and all the gathered information become one.

It is easier to have his hopes and think his way if one expects physics to be able to answer questions that are metaphysical. But even within physics, answers are harder to come by. For example, the recent and undeniable evidence that the known universe is expanding and is doing so more and more rapidly. These are the kinds of findings that Tipler's imagined Omega-ed divinity is going to easily enfold. Tipler's *Physics of Immortality* (New York: Anchor Books, 1997) produces an emergent personal divinity that explains reality and gives meaning.

September 8

I am trying to take in the scope of transhumanism by looking at the aspirations that transhumanists such as Dyson and Tipler have for technology and the sciences. I see them as seeking to stave off death and its seeming inexorability. Since I do not believe they will be able to do this, I want to contrast their aspirations with those that believers have for afterlife. There is a kind of mimicry of it by transhumanism.

The new physics has learned things about space and time beyond what common sense knows about these. This knowledge is germane to the subject of afterlife since what space and time are for those who have died seems to be a legitimate question for those of us who believe in afterlife. I think Augustine's insight again pertains here: that our knowledge of God can increase if our knowledge of nature increases. And since natural science is learning more and more about nature, we have the opportunity of knowing more about nature's Author. Physics in particular is learning more and more about space and time. For example, there is also new evidence of the relation between life on earth and its emergence, namely that it came from chemical reactions brewing between the stars. "Not so long ago, deep space seemed static and dull; now it looks like the possible breeding ground for a blue-print of life that might be shared across all the universe." Although it seems now that molecular life began in outer space, it is not yet clear exactly how it got to our planet. "Life doesn't care about the 'Made in . . .' label on the molecules" (Andrew Grant, "From Cosmic Blue-Print of Life," *Discover*, November 2010, 44).

September 10

Many in physics are expecting that we will get to a unified field theory that will put together our knowledge of the fundamental ingredients and the elementary particles in our world. I believe this aspiration will always fall short of satisfactory since its a priori physical. "A theory of everything" will have to include a pneumatology, still to be further developed, that will have to include the high Christology in the New Testament. Especially promising here is the kind of understanding of Christ we find in the Letter to the Hebrews, which speaks of him as our leader and the forerunner of faith (Heb. 12:3).

Explaining how he was both of these needs two Christologies, not one to explain him.

Actually I believe these three directions—Christology, pneumatology, and a unified theory could be interwoven. The interweave of the three will be needed for a satisfactory theory of everything to be arrived at.

The epistemology of metaphor would be helpful to recall here since what we are seeking to explain will not be easily grasped. A good metaphor is useful for explaining things. Dance is a good metaphor to explain the interaction of the three Divine Persons. They are not a dance but by the same token their relationship would be less colorful and interesting if this metaphoric image of their interaction had not been articulated and allowed to play in the minds and hearts of believers for centuries.

A good metaphor invites imagination. Several, even more. How about Incarnation? Together they can keep our attention on the mystery and by thinking and acting, wondering and, finally, kneeling. A poor metaphor could make a false unity, a kind of "turtles all the way down" kind of thing. That won't do. But here we can access the incarnate, human, Jesus who, led by the Spirit, learned the dance steps that made and makes him a forerunner for our learning to be led by the same Spirit into the same dance.

September 13

A doubt could be raised that since both space-time and the afterlife are much more unknowns than knowns, trying to get further intelligibility about each of them by linking them together will produce even more obscurantism than if we stayed with just one of these two subjects. My hope is that obscurity about each will diminish by trying to understand one in light of the other.

[Handwritten note at top: If eternity is an endless now, the ceasing of time (change measurement), then those in eternity are changeless (no movement, no singing, no praising]

Insofar as space-time accompanies reality as we experience it now, and insofar as we entertain the hope that we will be transformed when the new creation comes—these two insofars leave us with two questions. One is to know better what space-time is now so that our expectations about our transformation might be more enlightened. The more we know about space-time now, the more intelligent our expectations about our and its transformation will be. Further levels of understanding space-time should lead to a clearer judgment about afterlife. (When corruptibility yields to incorruptibility, etc., space-time will have something of immortality to it.)

The second question is about the hopes that developed in believers when time was understood differently, which can now be judged negatively by us. Before physics and Einstein came along, time was imagined to be in effect an absolute duration. Consequently, one lived in hopes of an eternity that would begin after time. So time would cease with the person's entry into eternity. Time happened as one lived one's life, but when one expired, one lived in a new condition, an eternal one. For the dead, time expired. What happens to this picture when time and space are combined and lose their character as common sense had imagined them? Can we know more about afterlife if we know more about space-time? I hope so. What is it that we could know if we added some theological insight to it?

[Handwritten note in right margin: No change]

We should know that eternity, eternal life, begins within time not after time, and that the kingdom is not simply to come but can be experienced as a here-and-now kind of thing, and that the conditions of heaven are to begin, not when we enter a space other than here which has been called heaven, but that whatever it is is already somehow present in this space. We should also know enough about the incarnation to realize that it was God's unremitting commitment to space and time. Jesus' continuing to be a human being after his death by rising from the dead is still our best indication of this. His ascension was not an exodus from space and time but an invitation to not cling to him corporally and to embrace the whole mystery of him in all its height and depth, length and breadth, including time and space as our knowledge of these increases.

The sacraments, furthermore, are a special way of having our future and God's future coalesce in present space and time. They continually renew those who receive them as well as the space and time in which we live and move and have our being. A church structure occupies a particular space and time. It assists worshippers to develop a greater clarity about their meaning and to give meaning to the time and matter they occupy.

In the Genesis account God pronounced "good" what was created or what emerged from matter, that is, light, darkness, earth, vegetation, animals, humans. The Genesis story is told in terms of time—one day, then the next day, then the next till there are seven. With each new emergent, whether that's a matter of a day or billions of years, each needs room, a space to emerge into beyond that which is occupied by the previous moment. And Easter took place the first day of the week, the first day of the new creation! Accordingly and rightly so, Sundays have become sacrosanct in many places ever since, give or take a little. Like Jewish Sabbath days, they are meant to be a day of rest that is a renewing of beings in time and space. It was also the day that anticipated the eighth day of Creation when all would be at rest and renewed.

An ecclesial understanding becomes a misunderstanding if some space is considered sacred in a way that implicitly denigrates the rest. The same with time—some times are sacred, and other times meaningless. Space, time, and matter are all part of what God has called good, and evidently, this is how God intends the new creation to be. The new physics seems to bring light to the old faith and hope.

I find I am undergoing an intellectual conversion about time and space. It is about the place of afterlife and the factor of time in that "after." At this point *after* looks to the future; when the afterlife is experienced, there will be no past or future, only a now and only a here. Since space-time is now considered a single rather than a dual reality, these vectors, which are usually experienced as separate, will be relative to each other rather than separate from them. So there seem to be three changes necessary about these coordinates, one is to not see them merely through common sense; two is to not see them as separate; and three is to see them in light of afterlife. In all three cases we have to leave the familiar everyday world of common sense, of locales that our faith narratives have supplied. Faith that is always seeking understanding always has to stay open to the new understandings the finding of science supply.

Donald Polkinghorne's assertion is that God chooses to know the world in its becomingness and does so not looking at it from the outside in. This seems true from the self-bestowal of God on time and space and creation and eventually on humans and on Jesus in the Incarnation. This mystery seems germane to our understanding of space (here and now) and of time (now and for all eternity) which is here where the creation is (Polkinghorne, *Methodology for the Human Sciences: Systems of Inquiry*, 282–83 [SUNY Press, 1983]).

September 21

A Genesis 11:1–9 Poem
I reverence the stones on which the
    tower of Babel was built
Even more I respect their dismemberment.
I don't know whether this happened
    because of guts or God.
All I know is there have been sequels
And that we'll be participants in their next construction.

Erect is what we do; erectors are who we are.
History is one long construction, decon-
    struction, reconstruction.
It would be mindless to be moundless. But
    we have here no lasting tower.
And a stone will not remain on a stone
    "until it all comes true."
It can't displease the One who made us tower builders
that new towers of meaning keep getting constructed.
What seems needed is to be ready to exit
    them at a moment's notice,
The notice for their demolition is
    served by a breakthrough
into a new way of piling the stones
One upon the other. We can't live in yesterdays.
The height of the tower is what God had a
    problem with, so smaller towers of meaning
that can be dismantled seems to be the way to go.
If God were the Potter/Architect of it what
    would a godly tower look like?
I wonder how our need to build these towers
    would be affected if we knew
  that we are already the temple of God
    the Spirit of God inhabits.

September 27

Re: The Afterlife and Space-time
    With each new archaeological dig and paleoanthropological
discovery, our emergence into time as a species, our "whence"
in other words, gets a little clearer. But our individual and
collective *whither* isn't getting any clearer, since the dead don't
talk. I hope that our near universal aspirations for an afterlife,

on the one hand, and the aspirations of the sciences, including the discoveries of physics about space and time, on the other, have something to say to each other. The long human tradition of having aspirations about an afterlife needs to be revisited, given the new insights from physics into space and time. Since it has become *space-time*, is it possible to give this change a theological reading?

Knowledge about afterlife, of course, is largely a matter of hope, so I can't promise the moon by my inquiry. Does the now-understood unitary character of space-time have something to say about the afterlife? I do not mean that space and time are one and the same but that they are conjoined in ways that had eluded human perception until the beginning of the twentieth century when Albert Einstein posited their connectedness.

There are five issues to be sorted out. One, is to try to understand space-time. Two, is to learn what this tells us about who we humans are who live in space-time. Three, is to theologize about this new knowledge about the binary character of space-time. Four: what this might tell us about afterlife. Five: the intellectual conversions needed by physicists and scientists and theologians to put this information together.

Where we are isn't where we thought we were when space and time were seen as separate and laws unto themselves, as it were. Space had been seen as empty, a receptacle, extending *sine fine*. And time was just duration *sine fine*. For Isaac Newton space was boundless, static, and empty of anything except for the universal medium of ether. He was convinced that "the spirit is entangled" in this ether medium. I'm not sure what he meant by spirit, but he understood time as having started with creation and that it has kept ticking in somewhat measurable, constant ways ever since. Newton's main contribution had been about gravity, connecting the apple's fall from the tree and the earth orbiting around the sun. But with Einstein's drastic revision in the understanding of how space and time are wound tightly together, these two coordinates had to get beyond common sense and into theory, via his theory of relativity.

Where Newton had seen the law of gravity at work, Einstein's equations anticipated the curvature of space-time and the realization that there is a warping of time with space by matter and energy. So, for example, measuring something with a triangle on a flat space comes up to 180 degrees, but measuring something on the surface of a sphere is not the same.

Albert Einstein wasn't the first one with the insight into the coinciding of space and time, but he gave it its biggest push in 1905 with his theory of relativity. Gradually the world learned about the significance of the fact that all events obviously take place at a unique time and in a unique place but that a large part of its uniqueness is posited by the observers of the events.

Establishing the curvature of space-time via relativity pries open one's commonsense observation through the senses. When theories are developed and verified, we learn more about nature than our sense experience delivers. Ever since space-time as twinned came to be known, knowledge of the cosmos and nature has grown exponentially.

Ignorance about nature is also ignorance about God and in turn about ourselves. Even though we don't experience space-time as coincident, it is a mistake to imagine it as merely a scientific, theoretical thesis. It is nature and nature better understood, hence not circumscribed by subjectivism and anthropomorphism and geocentrism. With the realization that an object viewed has to take into account the mind of the measurer who is in the motion of space-time matters. The measurer is not just a measurer, he or she is an interpreter. Though we can appreciate how each human being experiences each event differently, physics as such isn't interested in what the subjectivity of the subject is bringing to it. But consciousness, even that of the most objective scientist, is not a tabula rasa. It is bringing something of its peculiar idiosyncrasy to the perception of any event.

The space we occupy in this universe is becoming bewildering because of what we are learning about our planet and other "heavenly" bodies as well. They are expanding inexorably and exponentially. Only slowly have we moved beyond a geocentrism (our earth as center of the universe) and are now finding ourselves challenged by a geo-fugalism, I guess you could say, almost lost in the near infinity of the just becoming known universe. And as the planets get further apart presumably space-time itself expands. Was there anything there before "the where" into which the expansion is now expanding? Is space-time created? Is there such a thing as empty space? Is the expansion of planets and galaxies into "outer space" an instance of new creation?

What we have learned about space-time is the sheer immensity, the near infinity of it. If an arrow unaffected by gravity were shot into space, it would go into this infinity if it had the lift and if it weren't intercepted. Two things would intercept it. One, it is likely to hit something because there are believed to be a hundred thousand million galaxies out there with each galaxy containing some hundred thousand million stars. Two, it will curve because of gravity. We used to think of space as a nothing between somethings, as a vacuum, in other words, with occasional objects exceptions to the vacuum. We now know not only that space is curved with time but also that within the universe there are at least three other mysterious realities that our arrow would have to negotiate: dark matter, dark energy, and black holes. Dark matter is a major unknown. More is known about black holes, but they are no less bewilderings. Black because they swallow light. If something gets too close to these star-eating light killers, it will be unable to escape the hole's gravitational grip, and it will never be seen again.

And since the universe is expanding, there must have been
a time when there was virtually no space between earth and
the sun and galaxies, but all of it was a tight ball of matter
and energy. This is how the Big Bang idea originated. With
the expansion piece now verified, the conception of a timeless,
spaceless intensely woven beginning point which burst into a
universe was an inevitable idea. Its starting time, if time is even
relevant here, was somewhere between 13.7 billion years and
15 billion years ago. The size of the matter in the bang, some
physicists say, was zero, although that is hard to imagine. If
it started from zero might it compress back to zero? Where
does gravity figure into this? And the curvature of space and
time? The physicists are on a hunt for a grand unified theory
to answer these questions.

I understand how physics has come to understand space
and time as inseparable and that four coordinates, not three,
have to be accounted for, one temporal (duration), and three
spatial (extension)—length (longitude), breadth (latitude), and
height (altitude). By the same token I can't say the equations
and mathematics entailed in the space-time construal are clear.
But space-time as coordinates radically rearranges what I had
come to believe about afterlife in my childhood images about it.

September 30

Our knowledge of the universe, its origin, its destiny, is still very
much at an early stage. We are only gradually learning to walk
and talk, think and speak within space-time. As the universe
is seen to expand, so is thinking. But the deeper our probes
into the physical universe, the more its secrets get revealed
and simultaneously concealed. Three darks are revealed—dark
matter, dark energy, dark fluid. Concealed: what they are.
Also, what is Einstein's cosmological constant—the mysterious

pushes and pulls of various kinds of gravity. Then there are "bubble universes," which supposedly predated ours but are contemporary with ours. But even to call the universe "ours" is far too parochial, since there are an estimated 100 billion galaxies, if we can believe what astronomical instruments have accessed. So, the *uni* in the word *universe* is becoming more an imaginary infinite than a conceivable thing.

The *whence* and *whither* of our humanity are questions physics alone won't answer even though it is continuing to contribute to its depth chart. It promises an intelligibility it hasn't delivered and won't of itself. A Nobel Prize winner in physics, Steven Weinberg, whose book *The First Three Minutes* comments about the findings of his discipline: "The more the universe seems comprehensible, the more it seems pointless" (*The First Three Minutes: A Modern View of the Universe* [Basic Books, 1993]).

The more physics one learns, the more one's appetite is whetted to get from description to explanation to meaning. Two of the major theories in physics remain unintegrated. Quantum mechanics is king in the microworld. Relativity theory is king of the macroworld. Neither one is easily or ever fully grasped, even less their connection. Nor is it likely that a satisfactory meaning about who we are will come from either of these two theories, alone or together.

The commonsense meaning about space and time is available to one and all. But grasping space-time, that is, these two components tied to one another, is not obvious in itself nor is it for our meaning or "our" universe's. Like information, space-time has a unique kind of being. Furthermore, it is as ubiquitous as being. As far as we can understand, whatever has being must have being in space-time.

To take them one by one: commonsense meaning about time: as I experience myself growing older, I am able to become present to the past through memory and to the future through hopes, intentions, and goals. Even in the face of our mortality, the majority of humans seems to entertain a hope to get from being in this time to being in a time imagined to not end, an eternity of time. Further, throughout history people and their cultures have had an intuition about or made a differentiation between chronological time and *kairos* time. *Chronos* time is tick-tock time. *Kairos* time is experienced as timeless; it has an eternity to it.

Telling time in the cosmos isn't the slam dunk it was before space was pierced with rockets and satellites and planes because time on these devices doesn't register what it does on the ground one left from. Nowhere is time now the same. There is no universal "now" now. Odd as it may seem, the cosmic micro radiation that was emitted from the Big Bang 13 billion 700 million years ago is detectable today. A more immediate reminder of the oddity of time: one can enter into the future by flying into tomorrow by plane without living out today, or one can travel back into yesterday for that matter via the same conveyance.

About space: in almost every city or village humans have inhabited they have made some places sacred so that they can connect themselves to eternity via a particular space, the sacred localized. The felt need has been to capture the beyond by making a space sacred. One thinks of Peter's impulse at the scene of the Transfiguration: "let us build three tents here."

And within space there's the mystery of the darks already alluded to. What we thought we knew about gravity and matter itself, the reality of dark matter manages to confuse. The galaxies are now found to be rotating faster than the laws of gravity can explain. Dr. Vera Rubin, an astronomer at the Carnegie Institute of Washington, a specialist in "terrestrial magnetism," who has helped make dark matter a major issue in physics, has been quoted as saying: "I don't know if we have dark matter or have to nudge Newton's Laws or what. I'm sorry I know so little; I'm sorry we know so little. But that's kind of fun, isn't it" (Dennis Overbye, "The Joy of Physics," *New York Times,* December 29, 2009).

October 3

God is said to "tell the number of the stars and call each by name" (Ps. 147:3–4). Astronomy is only now finding out what kind of numbers God could tell us, realizing that we have been guilty of a serious "undercounting" of their number in the universe. We are learning that we have to stop using the Milky Way as a template for understanding the rest of the universe. The Milky Way had been taken to be the measure of other galaxies, but now we have knowledge of eight other "nearby" galaxies, each of which consists of 100 billion stars each—and that's just for starters. It was one thing to get past our geocentrism with the help of Copernicus and Galileo, but now it seems we even have to try to get over our galactic-centric way of thinking.

Cosmological factoids can make one dizzy. Technology helps us see how little we know about what we thought we knew. As nature unfolds its secrets, it is easy to lose one's footing as prior meanings seem to become obsolete. It would seem that without developing a theology of nature to complement our growing knowledge of nature, our knowledge could make us either mute about God or numb about meaning.

One of the wonders of physics is that it keeps inviting us beyond yesterday's findings into new ever more capacious hypotheses and theories. It is a rapidly evolving discipline with a history of orphaning its last set of parents as it moves beyond yesterday's knowledge to new findings and hypotheses. One author, Stephen Barr, a physicist from the University of Delaware, gives one a bird's-eye view of some of these orphaning moments. (A) The universe didn't have a beginning until the twentieth century pretty much proved there was a Big Bang. (B) The laws of nature anticipated that we could predict the next series of findings until the laws of physics with its quantum electrodynamics has begun to make everything untidy. (C) *Homo sapiens* seemed like a fluke of emergence until the confluence of the findings of physics makes *anthropos* (us) seem much less flukey. (D) It is only a matter of time before the computer and artificial intelligence will master the world of information, at which time human intelligence will come to appreciate the inimitability of and the dimensionality of the mind. (E) We are moving beyond the determinism of earlier physics into the indeterminism of quantum. In general, Barr has an appreciation of the unstoppability of the mind to ask new questions and come to new insights that keep unsettling those minds that have tried to settle their questions with scientific understandings alone (*Modern Physics and Ancient Faith* [University of Notre Dame Press, 2006], 26).

October 5

The more cosmology one learns, the more explanations one needs. The unexpected and explanation need each other. To be anecdotal about this and cite one experience that dazzled me: It was from viewing the Imax 3D Hubble documentary at Washington's Air and Space Museum. First of all, experiencing the magnitude and beauty of the heavens that instrument was able to glimpse. Another aspect of it was the degree of genius that went into constructing the instrument. A third was the discipline, courage, and know-how of the crew that could successfully fix the broken part of the Hubble capsule by exiting the confines of it 320 miles above planet earth tethered to their space capsule by only a small cord.

While marveling at that cosmic panorama, I recalled a line in one of e e cummings poem's: "so who cares if some one-eyed son-of-a-bitch has invented an instrument to measure spring with." Who cares? We all care, presumably, since the instrument enables us to see deeper into "spring," as it were, as no previous generation of human beings has ever been able to see before Hubble. This increases wonder not only about how minuscule earth and we earthlings are within the universe but also how unique we seem to be for developing the knowledge to construct something as complex as that instrument to come to more knowledge.

Hubble itself is a vivid reminder of the human appetite for *more* that humans carry in their psyches. We are constitutively vectored toward a beyond and not just of space and time, but for explanation and meaning. We become befuddled if explanation and meaning are not attained. It does not seem possible to glimpse the fact of the universe, its magnitude and silence and power and beauty and violence, and settle back into meanings about ourselves previously entertained.

Scientific findings make one marvel both at nature and human intelligence. Nonetheless, even as we come closer to understanding the mysteries of nature, we also know we aren't able to fully do so. New knowledge provokes new questions beyond yesterday's answers. At the same time this should force faith out of its old boundaries and into new ones and into an elasticity not previously needed. If one is already satisfied with the meanings about oneself and humans' and nature, fine. But if these are not enough, nonscientific disciplines such as theology can be a complementary, supplementary way of finding or framing further meaning. Theology presumes faith, and faith operates in the realm of transcendent meaning. So it presumes we continually need to connect the observed data with the meaning, which common sense and theory and theological theory can produce. Absent this and one will live in anomie or be satisfied living with meanings that can't be connected to one another, so with a faith disconnected from science and science from faith.

I want to reflect more theologically on space-time. What does knowledge about space-time, such as it is at the present time, say about the human proclivity to go beyond yesterday's meanings? Does theology have anything to contribute to this vast vista that is yawning out before us? Could it help provide some alignment between previous realms of meaning with ever-developing cosmological data?

October 8

In the course of trying to make sense of space and time and now space-time I am conscious of needing a particular virtue. In a chapter in a recent book I wrote, *Where Is Knowing Going?* (Georgetown University Press, 2009), I examined the virtue of hospitality. The more hospitality I can give space-time, the more its otherness enlarges my consciousness. Hospitality challenges and enriches. I liken the process to the need to have the space of a "commons" in the front of my consciousness where otherness or the stranger can enter and have its say or strut its stuff. The other can be persons or ideas or worldviews or horizons or other faiths. Here and now it is space-time that I am trying to invite into my commons, but its otherness is proving to be very ornery. I initially thought I could give it a home in me. Now I find I am the one needing to find my home in it. It is bringing me into its reality. The more I learn about it, the more I am tempted to pull up the oars of my mind and settle back into floating on the same old, same old that was familiar.

Making room for otherness is an achievement. And the more radically other the other is, the more one needs help to make room for it. Some otherness is more comfortable to invite into one's space and entertain than others. I began trying to be a good host of space-time, but found I am being invited to be its guest, hence having to obey its now-you-see-it-now-you-don't peculiarities. I started off walking into the data but soon had the feeling of tumbling. It's humbling how small one's humanity can feel within this vast and endless space-time we are finding in this strange universe. Nevertheless, we humans are able to give it something it can't give itself: i.e., names. So rather than being rendered mute, the challenge is to *name*. Gerard Manley Hopkins observed that nature can "only be"; it has "no tongue to plea, no heart to feel" (see his poem "Ribblesdale"). Physics and mathematics and astronomy and cosmology have all been exercises in finding and naming—as every discipline does—and will continue to be.

Since nature has no tongue, we need ours to name our relation to it in all of its parts. We humans are part of nature—in fact, emergents from within it. And nature seems to function as a unified whole without our intervention or our being able to understand how it does. Since believers are part of it, it behooves us to stay as literate as we can about it. It also behooves us to do our part to add to and not subtract from its incredibly complex operations.

Finding myself to be space-time's guest, the help I find I need for this task of naming is faith—faith in two senses. One is faith in science, its quest, its questions, its ability to hatch theories and test and empirically ground its hypotheses in ever-unfolding data. The other is faith in God who made space-time and equips minds to become capacious enough to take in this bulky otherness. The gift of faith enables believing, just as the gift of hope enables hoping, and love loving, and intelligence comes up with answers to questions. These gifts are key to helping meaning grow, here the meaning of the data of science to grow into a consonance with the realm of transcendent meaning and interiority. Faith generates the capacity to enfold the new into the old, and vice versa. In this case it's the ability to take in the coordinates of nature's space-time and do so in such a way that faith itself is transmogrified, and humans can continue on with the challenge of believing without seeing.

October 11

It's one thing to become literate about nature; it's another to develop insight into its meaning vis-à-vis us. As faith seeks understanding of cosmological data, it starts with questions. Some of mine about the material already mentioned are: (1) Before something material came to be was there space or time? (2) There would not have been a creator before anything was created, but did space-time in a sense make God the Creator? (3) Since creation presumes that space and time and God are contemporaries in a way, does that make space God's space in the subjective genitive sense of it and God's time? It would seem so, since believers have experienced themselves as able to enter God's space via their acts of faith, hope, and love, which enable believers to have a sense of God in our space-time and our space-time in God. (4) Is there such a thing as outside of time? or another space and time? such as where the dead go after they depart this space and time? (5) Will space-time cease to be? (6) How could it if there is a "resurrection of the body," since a body has to be in space somehow? (7) Will what has come into being necessarily cease to be? or can there be a "lived happily ever after" connection between the Maker and the made, i.e., here, in this space-time? (8) Since science anticipates the end of the universe as a scientific factoid (the second law of thermodynamics is that stuff runs down and out), where would an "eternity" take place? (9) Can anything continue to be without space-time accompanying it? (10) Is the universe then just a debris-to-be thing in the social imaginary of the afterlife of traditional belief?

Religion has always taken space and time for granted. The many religious metanarratives that developed during the first axial period (ca. 800 BCE–200 CE) were composed when knowledge of space and time was prescientific. Since sophisticated cosmology and physics came on the scene, it is better and more credible for the religions to understand and teach their faith stories within the frame of updated knowledge. A consonance between faith and reason is ideal when one reinforces the other. When they don't, faith weakens or disappears.

[handwritten margin note:] 3 rd axial period

Trying to construct a theology of space-time is not the same as trying to use reason on empirical data to prove God exists. The scientist goes about her work with a particular curiosity and hypothesis and with a subjectivity constantly trying to interpret empirical data. The theologian goes about her work the same way but with a penchant for a heuristic explanation, not for an empirical verification. Science comes up with much data and many explanations but is not likely to arrive at sufficient explanations since most of our questions seek meta-empirical answers.

Biblical stories, of course, are told within the framework of space and time, but they tell us little about space and time as coordinates. So one ends up ignorant or should become formally agnostic about what the Bible implies about these cosmological coordinates. And even within the relatively brief time of the Bible's construction its space and time categories do a lot of shifting. The Old Testament's cosmologies depended on who was in their neighborhood or whose neighborhood the Israelites were in. The usual biblical image of the cosmos was three-tiered, with Sheol a shadowy world underneath and with "the heavens" up above the middle tier of earth in which humans lived and to which some of them might be fortunate enough to climb beyond (Amos 9:2).

In the New Testament, too, the cosmologies are always
local and at the same time indeterminate. There was a Hades,
according to Luke's Jesus and a heaven to which Mark's Jesus
is taken up and within which he is now seated at the right hand
of God. Matthew's Magi knew that someone great had been
born under a star's luminescence (2:1). All of this framing has
to be differentiated from what the contents of the revelation
are. It has taken centuries to see that the biblical framing is
negotiable and that a reframing is legitimate, even necessary,
if space-time physics and faith are to be seen as compatible.

October 13

In particular, Hell—or Sheol or Hades or Gehenna—merits
some mention here. "Gehenna" is mentioned seven times in
Mark, once in Luke, and once in John. In the New Testament it is a place, a rubbish heap at the edge of the old city of
Jerusalem. It is a valley Jews called *Ge Hinnon*. Jesus and his
hearers would have associated the place in their minds with
fire, doom, a place into which infidels, sinners, the wicked are
cast. It was a cursed place.

Since the cosmological boundaries within which Christian
faith has been understood have to be redrawn, what shape or
frame should they now take? God out there, up there, and
heaven up there too and hell down there, and world here and
now—these are all erstwhile localizations of cosmological and
personal and collective identity and don't have the cachet they
had anymore.

"Heaven" and Hell were important spaces or places in the
prescientific Christian worldview. But scriptural revelation has
to differentiate itself from these imagined localizations.

Space and time questions were asked of Jesus in the Gospels.
Like Thomas's at the end of Jesus' ministry: "Where are you

going?" (John 14:5). He answers that he is the where of God. I am the way (there), the truth (of where God is), and the life (of God) (John 14:6). At the beginning of his ministry the question put to him was: "Where do you live"? (John 1:38). His answer was: "Come and see!" (v. 39). It would be ideal, of course, to be able to enter God's space by undertaking the same seeking and finding that Peter and John experienced. Presumably Jesus himself gradually learned to be at home in God's space. Eventually, his answer to the *where is God* question was "I am."

And apparently the time issue was answered by him in the same way. When the crowd taunted him and claimed its identity was with Abraham, he denied they knew what they were talking about or that they had any relation to Israel's founding figure. He located himself on the contrary as senior to Abraham. "Before Abraham was, I am" (John 9:58). Allowing, as we must, for postresurrection inspiration for preresurrection dialogues, the statement still has an impact about time and him. He subsumed space and time questions into his own person. A lot there! He emptied himself into space and time with his incarnation and became their alpha and omega.

October 16

John Ruskin, the nineteenth-century art critic, says that "the greatest thing a human soul ever does in this world is to see something and tell what it saw in a plain way . . . to see clearly is poetry, prophecy and religion—all in one" (Alister E. McGrath, *A Fine-Tuned Universe* [Louisville: Westminster John Knox Press, 2009], 29). The great value of physics is its unrelenting empiricism, its tantalizing hypotheses and startling evidence. But it can fall into a cul-de-sac if not complemented by other disciplines, especially the discipline of theology about a faith that delivers something more complete and meaningful than physics has been able to provide.

Four theological themes from a Christian faith can have the effect of enchantment on a scientific mind. One is the resurrection, two is the new creation, three is a theology of communion, four is sacramental knowledge. These four can and for centuries have given humans the *trans*-cendence their hearts and minds have needed to look for more than empirical evidence supplies. These themes to be elaborated on here are ways of coming to meaning that space-time physics provokes but does not of itself generate.

The first theme is the resurrection. Believing the risen body of Jesus has risen, where has it risen to? Where is he now? Wherever he is, the bodily risen Christ can't be beyond space now since a body must be in a space. In what space is the hoped-for resurrection of the body of Christians in? Where is this? Of course, the body of Christ that the Christians believe they already are in and experience themselves to be part of is the beginning of an answer to the question. But it is not a sufficient one. What has to be done is to see that space-time itself is already getting transfigured. Mary's and Jesus' bodies are in a space-time that is transfigured by their being in that "there."

The Christian Creed professes belief "in the resurrection of the body and life everlasting. Amen!" Resurrection had been a latecomer category in the Hebrew Scriptures (e.g., 2 Macc. 7). But it moved front and center in the early Christian communities since they both believed and experienced that's what Jesus underwent. Belief in the resurrection of the body, beginning with Jesus, makes Christianity *sui generis* in the history of the religions.

And the extraordinary belief that there is bodily life after death was not the only tangible evidence Christians had to show for their belief in it. The fruits of the Spirit (Gal. 5:22–23), surfaced in the behavior of the living. St. Paul for one experienced the presence of the risen Christ embodied in the

Body of Christ

Christian community. Community is meant to be an anticipatory experience of the resurrection mediated through the flesh of believers here and now.

St. Paul pictured the first Adam and last Adam in space-time terms. Adam, the "first man was from the earth, earthly" but Jesus who became and still is flesh is "the last Adam, a life-giving spirit" (1 Cor. 15:45). To be one with the first man is to be of earth and to inherit corruption; to be attached to the second man enables one to "inherit incorruption" (v. 50). "Flesh and blood cannot inherit the kingdom of God" (v. 50). So how does one inherit this kingdom? By being in Christ who was and still is flesh but who was indwelt by Spirit during his life and was not abandoned by Spirit in his death. As with Jesus, so with us, the Spirit takes what is there and indwells it bringing it into a new condition, a condition that flesh would not otherwise inherit. That which is corruptible and mortal is raised incorruptible and immortal (vv. 53–54).

The way Paul sees it: "a natural body is put down (or sown) and a *spiritual* body comes up (or is raised)" (v. 44). Recent scholarship sees Luke intentionally commenting negatively on this "spiritual body" expression of Paul. With Jesus' appearance to the 11 on the first day of the week, the apostles thought they were seeing a ghost. But he said: "Why do such ideas cross your mind? Look at my hands and my feet; it is really I. Touch me and see that a ghost does not have flesh and bones as I do" (Luke 24:38–39). Look at me, I'm as human as I was; stop making a ghost of me!!! Flesh was raised then, and is now.

October 19

The second theme which can enchant a scientific mind is the new creation. Those who were baptized into Christ began to see themselves as already participating in the promised new creation. This new creation was aborning here and now; it was not somewhere else or in the wholly future. "The kingdom of heaven is at hand" (Matt. 4:13). This new here and now milieu was entered into by baptism. The Sovereign of this new creation was interested in being enthroned first in the hearts of the baptized. Though his sovereignty is over all of the biota and abiota, his preferred way of having his reign known is through the acknowledgment of the baptized about his and their relation to this Lord and by their confessing their eternal connectedness with him and nature.

Since created nature includes the structures of space-time, will they also be part of the new creation? There may be a very simple answer to this question by reflection on what Jesus asked—"Have you anything here to eat?" (Luke 24:41). He wanted them to know that though he had been raised from the dead, he was the same as he was before. He ate and drank with them then and there as he had done at the Last Supper. The new creation is not a wholly future thing. It begins by seeing present nature through a new lens with the light he supplies, here and now with the Spirit.

Paul suggests a helpful way of understanding what the new creation is. It is to be accessed empirically, as has already been mentioned. The fruits of the Spirit were unmistakably operating in his milieu—love, joy, peace, patience, kindness, generosity, faithfulness, gentleness and self-control" (Gal. 5:22–23). The followers of Jesus were the evidence of the new creation emerging from the Spirit present and embodied and obeyed (v. 25), not as a result of "the law" or out of a behavioral conformity (v. 18).

To introduce the theme of theology of communion, let me note that we are connected to nature in ways we hadn't known before the insights of quantum physics, special and general relativity theory, and space-time. All of these scientific insights weave us and nature much more closely. They

are insights into our connectedness to nature in all its local, material particularity. This is a daunting and steep challenge to those whose metanarratives had spiritualized their identities out of its relation to nature and its physicality or to those who prided themselves as "made for higher things." Instead we were made *of* these lower things and would be well advised to bring them and ourselves into an integration that names and lives in communion with nature.

Raimon Panikkar in his book *The Rhythm of Being* (Orbis Books, 2010) named and cogently argued for this same insight. He links the *cosmos* and the *theos* and the *anthropos* in an unbreakable unity. So our reality is able to see that we are "cosmotheandric"! The terrestrial and the divine and the human are "all in this together." This whole refuses to see these three separately. Consequently, we have to hatch a new *mythos* in order for the unitary character of these three within which we are embedded to be understood instead of over against any one of the three as our earlier ignorances and supernaturalistic biases construed ourselves. Panikkar's is one of a number of new theologies of creation which invite humans to exercise a stewardship within our sameness with nature rather than with an imagined superiority vis-à-vis nature. The new mythos has to produce a mediation between nature and God, one that ceases to exploit and begins to befriend it, since the new creation is aborning from it. The new creation is both a now and a future. As a social imaginary it can take the place heaven had.

October 22

The new physics and insights into nature such as space-time invite us to revisit our understanding of our relation to nature. In this we are like the early Christians who were invited to understand God in a new way. It took them till the fourth century before they could develop the categories needed to grasp the relations between God as those of Father, Son, and Spirit. The communion of the Divine Persons with one another can birth a new social imaginary about nature and God and humans in communion, one with the other two. Seeing God as One and Triune invites a further insight into the foundational character of being as relational. Reality as itself in communion and relational was not something Greek philosophy would have guessed.

Contemporary cosmology has enabled moderns to become more knowledgeable about the heavens, their depth and height, length and age, and about how tiny planet earth is. So we can take the cosmological data and see it in a new light much more capacious than physics can provide.

The fourth century Cappadocian theologians did not invent the term koinonia, communion. Like all previous generations of Christians they celebrated the Lord's supper repeatedly, ritually, in memory of Jesus' last supper with his disciples. Their obedience to his wishes changed their experience of one another and of Jesus, and of God. Their experience was neither wholly spiritual nor wholly physical nor wholly interpersonal, nor wholly personal. It was all four of these in a communion. It carried over into expressing itself materially—a sharing of their personal goods with one another (Acts 2:44–45). Theirs was a "fellowship," an experience of themselves and Him in communion with one another. It was a faith experience, a hope experience, and a love experience. Where divinity stopped and humanity began was now a koinonia, a communion of God and followers of Christ, all of them with God through, with, and in Christ.

But this understanding of God as a Trinity of Persons-in-Communion who in turn is an ecclesial communion also needs to be made into a communion with the things of nature and of time and space and space-time. What is it that enables us to make these connections with nature's space-time/matter/energy and our human consciousness? The Spirit! It is the same Spirit inviting us now to make a communion with all things as had enabled the author of the Prologue of John to make the audacious assertion that through the Logos "all things came to be, and apart from him nothing came to be" (John 1:3).

Thinking Trinitarian thoughts is as difficult as thinking space-time thoughts. Valuable as efforts in either direction might be, the Gospel of John has one scene that might help. Jesus was aware of how localized the understanding of God usually is and certainly is in the case of the Samaritan woman at the well. He teaches her: "God is Spirit!" (John 4:24). But he goes further, and promises that a source of unending understanding shall be poured out like water. It will come from within her and many out into the world through them. They will be worshippers who will make the connections that the world needs and will eventually make. At the end of their dramatic tête-à-tête Jesus promises her: "Woman, believe me, the hour is coming when you will worship the Father neither on this mountain nor in Jerusalem. . . . but in Spirit and in truth" (vv. 21–23).

How will this happen? "The water that I will give will become in them a spring of water gushing up to eternal life" (v. 14) to those who are thirsty for understanding. Because of this, the water he will give which is the Spirit he and the Father will pour out, they, the recipients "will never be thirsty" (v. 14). Why won't they? Because their worship and understandings are connected. "God is Spirit, and those who worship him must worship in Spirit and in truth" (v. 24). The Spirit is the Connector within the Trinity and in the world; worship and understanding connect where the Spirit is at work.

The fourth theme is sacramental knowledge. The sacraments are the special way of having our future and God's future coalesce in the space-time of the present. They renew those who receive them as well as the space-time in which they necessarily take place. A church structure occupies a particular space and time. It assists worshippers to develop a greater clarity about their meaning as well as about all the rest of space and time and matter they occupy and have responsibility for.

Easter took place the first day of the week, the first day of the new creation! Accordingly and rightly so, Sundays for Christians have been sacrosanct. Sundays are the new Sabbath days. They are to be a day of rest that is renewing of beings in time and space. Every sacrament is meant to give us a whiff of an experience of the eighth day of Creation when the new creation will be all in all.

Every sacrament is constituted by something material, whether oil or water or bread or wine. In the Genesis account God pronounced "good" of what was created or of what emerged from matter, i.e. light, darkness, earth, vegetation, animals, humans—oil, water, bread, wine. "Good" was a pronouncement about then and now and for all time. The Genesis story is not only about material reality; it can also be read in space-time terms—one day, then the next day, then the next till there are seven. Good is pronounced also of space and time. With each new emergent, whether it's a matter of the space or time or of space-time, both together need more and more time that is now counted in billions of years, and more and more space is now understood to expand bewilderingly faster and faster with the expansion of the planets. Space-time has the wherewithal to become as sacramental as any material or human reality seen in the light of God is able to be.

One human proclivity that keeps material or human reality from being sacramental is to constrict it to just some spaces, such as a church, or to some times, such as the time of the celebration of the sacraments, or to just to one community, such as Catholics. An ecclesiology as well as an ecclesial understanding of communion and of sacramentality can become a source of misunderstanding if those who celebrate it constrict it by arrogating just certain spaces and times and bodies to be sacred while implicitly or explicitly denigrating what is outside of them as lacking sacredness or being meaningless or not possessing the goodness God has pronounced on them. Space, time, and matter are all part of what God has called good and as far as we know what God intends the new creation to be. It is not within our authority to limit sacramentality to what we in our narrowness deem or pronounce as sacred.

I end the "four themes" here conscious of the wonder of it all. Not thinking about space-time in its dimensions but content just to sit in the wonder of our being ensconced in it. Yes, there is always the need to know more about it and about physics but also to rest in the wonder of it all. The usefulness of wonder is that it makes one a child again; that may be the best use we can make of our consciousness. It does have other uses, of course; it moves scientists to go back to work on the next theory or experiment seeking more and more knowledge. And for us nonscientists we can mull their data and, hopefully, see it in a new way. Like sacramentally!

Seeing in a new way entails prayer. Whether personal, Eucharistic, or group prayer, all have this similarity: they are efforts at entering into the space-time of God. Occasionally space-time all but disappears in prayer. To take just one of these forms of prayer, Eucharist. The subject makes me think about the difference between belief and experience. I believe that the community's coming together to "do this in memory of me" makes the last supper Jesus had with his disciples and its redemptive import become present.

Notice! I believe this. Experiencing it is not the same. I want to experience his and their redeeming presence, but the experience of Mass is complex, personal, diffuse, often distracted. Eucharist is an event in which those who receive the body and the blood are being brought into the *already begun* communion of the new creation. But experiencing being in communion with members of the present recipient community is not a certainty. The more likely experience is of an all-over-the-place bunch of worshipers and an all-over-the-place worshipper, me—rather than a sacramentally alert worshipper and a community in communion with one another and the Trinity.

So, unfortunately, believing is not seeing. Beliefs are usually experienced more as hopes than as "seen." The best we can do religiously is to see as through a glass darkly. Beliefs bring us into a degree of communion with God. Prayer makes communion more likely and beliefs more believable and the future more present . . . and all of these more or less.

To go back to the curvature of space-time, which the new physics has pretty much taken as proven. It invites a new imaginary about the afterlife. Rather than leaving nature, those who believe in an afterlife can take this new knowledge about space-time and imagine the afterlife as curving back and taking place within the boundaries of nature. What adds cogency to this is what is called "realized eschatology," that is, to be in Christ is to be in the new creation, already. In Him the "to be" is already a here and now. Although common sense still imagines the afterlife being beyond time and space, we can now critique what our senses tell us about space and time as physics and faith in a tandem are coming to understand this.

Several "practical" benefits could come from the intellectual conversion that space-time now invites. One is that it would be hugely beneficial to nature if the human denizens who live within space-time and nature were to see themselves in communion with it rather than on their way to a home not here. A second benefit would be humility. The more we learn about things like how infinitesimal our planet is vis-à-vis the rest of the universe and the more we learn about how recent an entry we are in the lists of living things, human hubris becomes ludicrous. A third benefit would be for us to take more responsibility for our consciousness, what we fill it with and to what end? A fourth benefit would be a greater acceptance of the ebb and flow between knowledge and nescience, knowing and not knowing.

The dark night of the soul as experienced by the mystical tradition and its rare worthies mirrors the mystery of the dark matters physics runs up against in its quest for intelligibility. Physicists and mystics seem to have to deal with a similar temptation to desolation, that is, to wonder whether their quest is pointless. Or maybe the dark that's encountered in both cases is inviting the observers to slow down into a mode of waiting so that the "object" can speak more clearly for itself, if it chooses to.

Gateby
Week 50

October 25

I feel like I am being invited by God to lose my faith, not faith in God but faith in an understanding that has been far too small, boundaried, anthropocentric, ignorant. One thing that has been triggering this sentiment is the aspirational direction of the World Transhumanist Association. It encourages a replacement of religion by imagining humanity's capacities for constructing its own well-being via technology and science. The aspirations of that association open up one's imagination, but on reflection one has to become suspicious. It's in the right direction, since transcending limitations has always been what humans have aspired to, but its particular version of this human élan jumps off the rim of the real into a secularist never-never land.

Religion and a material naturalism have always to face off on each other. My understanding is that traditional Christian faith has not been sufficiently aligned with nature. If we were more sensitive ecologically, and more educated biologically, not to mention in physics and chemistry and neuroscience, this misalignment would diminish, maybe even be eradicated. Or to put the task another way: our social imaginaries are too narrow, our metanarratives too insular, our religions too supernatural, our knowledge of science too superficial. We have emerged from nature and as humans we are part of nature and whatever our future is will still be in some kind of communion with the nature of which we are a constitutive part. So how does this fit with traditional Christianity's view of afterlife as an elsewhere? The nexus between these two subjects, nature and afterlife, seems to ask for more than a mutual ignoring of one another.

Can any insight come from matters of such diversity? Let me try here. Obviously, space-time itself continues after someone or something or some species or some star expires. It had a past, has a present, and will have a future. If it doesn't, there would only be spacelessness, timelessness, nothing. Obviously space-time is and is a singular reality. One of its most obvious characteristics is that it "makes room" for everything that enters it. As far as we can tell, everything exists in space-time. By the same token, space-time is part and parcel of what is. In some ways its behavior seems to reflect or even imitate the behavior of the Spirit. It bears witness to the Spirit.

Again, if the better we know nature, the better we will know God, then the less we know what is knowable about nature, our knowledge of God will be proportionately deficient. It is this linkage that I am evoking here. Space-time is a difficult knowable since it virtually ignores the senses.

But so does Ruach or Pneuma. Jesus even seems to have complained about Spirit that you don't know whence it has come nor where it is going (John 3:8), Space-time and Spirit are similar in that way. They both elude the captivity of concepts, or conceptualization, being imageless. Incarnate they are not, but all-embracing they both are. How odd! Jesus, of course, wasn't talking about space-time as we know it now but about the space-time of the kingdom of God. And entry into that peculiar reality was via "water and Spirit; flesh begets flesh, Spirit begets Spirit" (vv. 5–6).

On the occasion of the twentieth anniversary of the death of Pedro Arrupe in 2011, a letter with three imperatives was sent to the whole Jesuit order by the Jesuit Superior General Adolpho Nicolas, asking individual Jesuits to pray over and take the measure of themselves from. Total cooperation was the third of these imperatives, and total immersion was the second of his imperatives, and total detachment was the first of these. When I look at what science is saying about nature, in particular about space-time, I take these three imperatives to heart. Immersion in the data, detachment from my prescientific ignorance, and cooperation with the small degree of connection between science and faith I can come up with. Space-time invites immersion in new boundaries and detachment from the old ones, boundaries that were laid out when ignorance was a kind of bliss.

There will be a moment when all of *being* transmogrifies into a new condition, when "God will be all in all," but if the incarnation means what we have believed it means, that prospective unitary reality will include matter, materiality, consciousness, and space-time. That makes me realize that space-time at the present has a sacramental kind of reality and therefore a role to play now in our world, which will become transfigured and more transparent in the future.

Everything present potentially has sign value for those who believe. Space-time has its own peculiar present reality but is almost as elusive as God is. Letting myself be present to its omnipresent otherness reflects the otherness of God's omnipresence. Just as the bread and wine have sign value, so space-time too has sign value. Pointing to what? The omnipresence of God and the omnipresence of space-time continue to intrigue me with their similarities. Both are always making room for here and now, and giving time to be present with and to, while never ceasing to be themselves and enfolding within themselves what is in all of its particularities, letting them be and become themselves. God has made a surrogate, it seems, of space-time. Track one and you find the other.

Space-time has an eschatological dimension to it, an "already" that isn't going to become extinct. If there is going to be the resurrection of the body, space-time will continue, because that's the condition within which bodies *are*. If we believe in an afterlife, it seems that we have to believe in space-time having some part of it. It seems it will be as pervasive then as it is now, if we are right to believe in the body's resurrection.

I remember asking a Congolese Jesuit what his tribe's experience was about where their dead go. Without a moment's hesitation he said, "They are in the same place we are, and where our bushes and trees, the fields and the flowers are. We experience them as present to us." The space-time coordinates physics has learned of are already part and parcel of their experience without their ever having heard of this sophisticated concept. Why their depth perception sees what more educated peoples do not see can be chalked up to superstition on their part or to the price we pay for the imagined sophistication we in the West are narrowed by.

October 30

What Does the Trinity Do When It Is Off Work?
It ones—a verb
(don't start partitioning this into parti-
    ciples or twisting it into tenses)
Their one-ing began with Three from the begin-
    ning and never stops being thus—
the Trinity is a mutual fund that continues
    to grow, a Trifecta of mutuality.

I believe in One God as an Act not as a finished
    given or a solipsistic substance.
When the Trinity goes back to work, the
    work it had rested from resumes.
Their work is then "that all might be
    one even as We are one" . . .
(Here one could go in one of two directions:
grieving about the ways we fall short of Their agenda
Or forget about that and the mess we
    all make of one-ing and
enjoy the One God is and becomes since
    that's what the God-self does . . .)

Our mirror neurons show that we are
more likely to do what we notice is being done.
So the more we notice God one-ing,
    the more likely we will become a human reflection of it
Otherwise we continue on, un-oned.
But since everyone of us hopes
    to-become-one and indeed,
for the lot of us to-become-one,
Then if the One has Its way with us we will!

November 3

The Prodigality of the Prodigal's Father
He ran; he ran all the way to his son.
There had been the prior run—the son's.
It ended when "the pigs are doing
    better than I am doing"
What's not to know about the second runner's heart—
The kiss, the ring, the robe, the fatted calf, the shoes—

That, unlike ours, it can be given
    totally to more than one,
Unconditionally!
He celebrates his son's choice to be back
And disallows an identity born of guilt.
As far as the east is from the west, that's
    how far the past is from his mind.
Then there is the second son.
"Everything I have is yours, always
    has been, always will be"
 How unlike the Father, the sons! . . .
Two sons—one had "attached himself to one
    of the propertied class of the place"
the other to an obediential attitude of doing the things
he thought his father wanted of him;
both false self-understandings;
 both shaken out of them by love;
and invited into the one their Father does—
which is what? He runs and ones! . . .

I know a mother whose son was on drugs for years;
he was a shiftless prodigal
She didn't know why he didn't answer her weekly letters
She never stopped till he ran back home.
Lucky him who had someone who cared enough
to be moved by the same love as the prodigal's father.
And acted on it notwithstanding the silence.
The result is a success story, starting with the letters
And what moved their being written.
Today he is the letter writer.

November 8

How is one-ing done? It seems to have two ingredients, reason and faith; they have to be continually mixed to have "fresh bread." When Jesus talked about the one-ing that he believed God had in mind, he used the image of the reign of God. He saw each person having the ability to make fresh bread, both for themselves and others. That's what he did. The Gospels are the story of a successful baker and the best teacher of the art.

Faith in reason includes believing in one's own ability to think things through with right reasoning; having faith believes one has something to learn and something to say because there's never been a you before, with your package of experiences and understandings, as well as having faith in the ability of your reasoning to come to intelligibility; believing that a subjectivity can get to objectivity.

Faith in the reasonableness of faith in God has been the source of meaning for many in the past and for many now. Faith in God can come up with meaning even when meaning gets thin. Faith believes that prayer is not an exercise in solipsism, but hears and is heard.

Where does knowing go? It goes toward one-ing. It goes from the operations of consciousness that are natural to the real, to a transcending of the self via its operations of experience, and understanding, to insight, to verification of insight to yes, then choice, then action. We are all endowed with the ability to get from "I don't know" to "this is so." Getting to reality by one-ing, one by one is our primordial desire.

The reign of God is where our "it-is-so's" go, where scrutiny ends up with good judgment and where there is a consistency between idea and action, between getting to the true and acting on it. Is this too a-religious? I don't think so; we glorify God by doing what we were made in the image and likeness of God to do. Which is what? Right thinking and choosing.

If there is not faith in reasoning, one's own and the reasoning of others, then the bread one produces, if indeed there is any, will be flat, stale, and unprofitable both for oneself and others. There has to be faith in the ability to get from subjectivity to objectivity, and to believing objective reality can be attained and attaining it. If intelligence is not self-transcending, it stays mired. It would be good if we knew how our subjectivity works so as to be more trustworthy about what is so, real, true, the case.

Being faithful to the traditions of right reasoning does not mean simply repeating past contents or being deductive from the already known and believed. Required is an investment of knowers into past insights and to the bread already baked. Being faithful to and contributing to a tradition, whether an intellectual or a religious one, entails not only believing what it has learned but also appropriating it so that it grows, as insight into reality grows.

November 10

In some ways the Gospel of John can be read as answering a triple question. The first is the way to God, the second is the where of God, the third is the answer Jesus gave to both of these as his identity grew evident both to himself and to his hearers. The three become intertwined as answers in the fourteenth chapter of John where Jesus describes himself as the way and the Father as his destination. He then drops the spatial here/there component of his discourse and sees himself as already where the Father is: "I am in the Father and the Father is in me" (vv. 10–11).

Two things kept his disciples from being able to see this communion between Jesus and the Father. One was because the Spirit had not yet been sent to enable them to see. Another was that the sin of the world had created a barrier between their seeing the way and the where and the who of God. That sin had not yet been removed. The promise Jesus makes is that, pending an event that had not happened, he and his Father would come to those who are "true to my word" and "we will make our dwelling place with them" (v. 22).

After the Last Supper discourse, Jesus' crucifixion and death and resurrection take place. The denouement of the whole Gospel crests then with Thomas's going from unbelieving to believing. The way, the where, and the who of God are now accessed. After putting his finger into the holes of Jesus' hands and his hand into Jesus' side, Thomas exclaims "My Lord and My God" (John 20: 27–28). The fourth Gospel starts with the Logos seen with God and as God. It then proceeds to the Logos becoming flesh and as enfleshed in Jesus, and eventually as the words and deeds of the Father.

Access to this God takes place now for those to whom the word has been sent who will each experience their own "my Lord and my God."

November 11

The Patristics have much to add to Paul's theology of the Spirit. Basil of Caesarea's contribution to it was his insight into the Spirit as the Completer. Along with the two Gregories, Nyssa and Nazianzus, Basil kept the Church from falling into a Trinitarian substantialism or tritheism and brought a relational ontology of personhood to the Church as theology even before the Council of Constantinople was convoked.

The question I asked myself after writing an initial answer to the question: Where is Knowing Going? is: How does knowing get going? I have concluded that the Spirit is the reason that reason gets going. This Giver of Life gives life to the brain, which never stops operating, even during sleep.

The church has always affirmed the need to attribute to all three Divine Persons the actions that take place *extra Deum*, and that there is also a unique role for each Divine Person in these actions of God in creation and history and persons. In this text I have focused on the unique role of the Spirit in acts of knowledge.

The Spirit is preeminently God as immanent. And as immanent, the Spirit's role and mission is to teach us all things, including the truth about our interconnectedness with God and all being. St. Basil in one sentence suggests some of spiritual aspects of what the Spirit would teach us. "Knowledge of the future, understanding of mysteries, apprehension of hidden things, the distribution of wonderful gifts of heavenly citizenship, a place in the choir of angels, endless joy in the presence of God, becoming like God, and the highest of all desires, becoming God" (Basil of Caesarea, *On the Holy Spirit* [St. Vladimir's Seminary Press, 1980], chap. 9, #23).

The most audible evidence we have of the presence of the Spirit to human beings is their confession of God as "Abba." This name names the headwaters and principal font of God in creation. Another accessible source of evidence of the presence of the Spirit in persons is the way the fruits of this presence manifest the Spirit in their interpersonal relations. This self-effacing Person is happy to strut the stage in the gifts and fruits of those who have received these.

The doctrinal tradition has preferred to see the work of the Spirit as sanctifier. Sanctification of the elect had for centuries seemed like the preeminent achievement the Spirit intended. Be that as it may, pneumatology also needs to see the Spirit as Completer, as the interconnector of all that is. When it does, the sciences could then take their findings and theories and entertain the idea that the Spirit might be undergirding of the increasingly complex data of each of them. At present the data in all the sciences is becoming voluminous and disconnected. The Spirit is how it is connected. If that seems too religious, theology could clarify that what God makes, God intends to become more and more itself and autonomous though not independent. This would make evident to all the love the *Maker* has for the *made*. Love is the interest and intention of the Maker, and it has Him affected by the directions the made go in. This is what we have all learned about interpersonal love and can then extend it to how God's love works—that is, being affected by the loved.

Communion seems to be the long-range goal of the mission of the Spirit. The Spirit is a whole maker bringing all parts together. Emergence into communion is slow but sure—i.e., the direction the Spirit is going in is one of connecting. It took millions of years for hydrogen and oxygen to come together. What emerges is new as the separate ingredients are gathered to make the new, like *Homo sapiens*. If there is one adjective that befits the way the Spirit works besides *Holy*, it is *Whole-making*.

Older wholes keep ceding to further, newer ones. How to explain the history of whole-making—even at the most minute subatomic level and then at the animal and on to the human level, to the interpersonal to the societal level and from there to the civic and the international level and to the universe itself? One whole-making cause would be one explanation of this. And Spirit could be brought forward as that cause. The disconnection between theology and science needs to be superseded so that these two areas of knowledge can bring new insight and energy to each other. The dialogue would be fruitful both for people of faith and people whose worldview is formed by or specialized in science.

November 13

In Genesis 2:7 we have an empirical kind picture of "the Lord God" taking the clay of the ground and forming one entity by blowing into its nostrils "the breath of life and so man became a living being." This picture might be another way for understanding wholes. For a long time we humans have been trying to put together scientifically the successive moments and constitutive parts of our emergence and constitution as humans. This breath of God might be a good addition and image in doing the science of the move from nonliving to living, and from prehuman to human, from "first parents" to the sprawl we are now. It would obviously not cancel out the need for science. By the same token, science would do well to revisit its findings and explanations and see that "spirit" in some form of the conceptualization of it has been in the mix of explanations for a long time. Otherwise unanswerable questions are still being asked and left unanswered. The prescientific character of the answers that ancients gave to their questions does not make them ignorant any more than our scientific answers have made us wise. Both have developed from the same intellectual capacities that all religious traditions of believing in God developed from.

The followers of Jesus of Nazareth found that he interrupted their experience both of God and of themselves. Therefore, they began to develop a series of formal beliefs about him, one of which was that the Spirit that came to rest on him, explained him to himself and also was explaining them to themselves. Further developments of this belief produced by the Spirit elaborated an understanding of God that was able to make a whole of God as Principle and Jesus as his Son. But as Father and Son came to be seen more and more, a third party emerged, which was Itself in them but was neither of them, therefore, distinct. This experience led to knowing the Spirit who came to be seen as a person, but unlike any other person human or divine.

Insight into the Spirit gradually emerges, connecting what would otherwise never have been connected, that is, earth and life, humanity and divinity, a divinity as Triune. I think of the Annunciation as the first scene of connection, of God with a human, a blastocyst in a womb, an angel announcing to a people its awaited Messiah, a scripture with a divine plan with its initial execution. The Spirit in this annunciation scene is an angel, both transcendent yet immanent, and reverently sensitive about Mary's autonomy but inexorable about connecting what otherwise would have remained apart. In this scene we have a tangible image of both the mission and the style of the Spirit. Granted, this does not come close to fully understanding the Spirit, but it jump-starts our understanding of its mission as connector and for centuries has triggered our imaginations and expectations.

Another way of imagining this Connector is to start with how we imagine nature started, namely from the big bang and go from there to quarks to stars to planets to the formation of earth to nonliving things to living things, and to humans, to us, alive and kicking. There are many ways of perceiving this emergence, but notice the connectivity that flows from one stage of being to the next. The new emergent depends on the old and on its component parts without the former having within itself the ingredients to explain how the subsequent one developed.

November 16

What makes more and more sense is the belief that the Spirit has been accompanying the workings of nature and human nature and of human intelligence in the entire course of their evolution. The recognition of this Divine Person carrying out Its mission reverently for all the component parts of nature can generate awe about It. Yet the Spirit seems never to have been in a rush or have had a need to be recognized, since Its presence has largely not been recognized, at least as Spirit, as we are coming to understand It. Ironically, in this we are becoming more like our forebears, the many early peoples who recognized and worshipped in many different ways a numinous presence in nature.

Although a transhuman causality was recognized by our human ancestors from the earliest times as archaeological, anthropological, and historical studies of their practices of worship have unearthed, we moderns might be becoming so full of knowledge that we do not see what our forebears saw. What will it take for us to come to a recognition of the trans-human, divine factor operating in nature and human nature notwithstanding Its self-effacing character?

This transhuman component could be more easily seen as Spirit if there were a willingness on the part of theologians to be engaged with and informed by what the sciences have been learning about every history and matter. While there's so much more that we know now than was known especially before modern science's findings, a religious insight needs to be seen of something whole emerging from the parts. Both science and religion have much to teach each other. Neither, of course, will learn from one another if the practitioners don't believe each has something important to say.

November 20

Matter was perennially seen as inert and only able to be shaped by something immaterial like form in Plato, entelechy in Aristotle, soul in traditional Christianity, or mind, life, thought, knowledge in the course of the history of civilization. One complicating factor in philosophy's demotion of matter to its place of relative insignificance was Descartes's dualism. He posited two mutually exclusive ontological categories—*res extensa* and *res cogitans*, material being and thinking being. Therefore, insofar as the world became Cartesian, the Spirit would have to qualify under the category of and in the realm of *res cogitans*, mind, before its universal interconnectivity with all things and between and in material emergents could be weighed and recognized. The Spirit is no less reverent about matter than It is about mind, than it is about human freedom. Again I go back to the Annunciation scene to watch this aspect of how gently It executes its mission.

Much of modern theology has developed on a theological anthropology via the social sciences. But theological anthropology is relatively innocent of the natural sciences. So this theological anthropology has to be further developed through both the natural sciences and pneumatology. Doing so could make Christian anthropology a more capacious category and help it take its place in the universal discourse that is needed for our modern world.

Jesus bequeathed to his followers a personalized understanding of Spirit. He made the Spirit a Person even though Its personhood was unlike any other person his hearers could have ever imagined. The Person of Jesus is still so much more imaginable than the Spirit. Given the understandings about human personhood that have developed within the social and natural sciences, personhood is now more clearly understood as socially mediated and relational than it was when the distinctive Personhood of the Three Persons of the Trinity was being grasped by the early church. Human personhood is now better understood as a system of relations that are interwoven and interdependent genetically, neurologically, interpersonally, culturally, and, of course, historically. Just to mention one natural science, neuroscience: it has made our nexus with nature much richer and infinitely more complex than we had ever imagined when we were positing "personhood" of the Triune God.

Each Person of the Trinity was, of course, believed to be in the genre of a Divine Person and on a par with one another. But understanding the Spirit as Person is more dissimilar than the way of understanding the Father or the Son as Persons. The distinctiveness of the Spirit was/is better understood as the telos of the emergence of all that was, is, and will be connected than in isolation from it. The Spirit as the Author of revelation has entered into history and into our perception of It very slowly. It is as if perceiving God as Spirit is only now in-breaking in comparison with the time when linear notions of prime mover and efficient cause of what "has been and is and always shall be" ruled the day. The three Divine Persons are not in relation to one another in the same way, nor are they relating to creation in the same way nor to each of us in creation in the same way.

The undifferentiated attribution of anything simply to God always makes the different roles of the Persons of the Trinity in creation seem superfluous. There has been a theological neglect about the issue of attribution. The prepositions are key here, like *through* versus *in* versus *with*. Our Christology has rightly made the claim that all things were made through the Word, but it is in the Spirit that all things came to be and still come to be. While there is one divine nature, and all the divine actions vis-à-vis creation are one, still there is the proper role of each of the three Divine Persons.

For Christians the best sources for the revelation of the Spirit are still the events of the Annunciation, Baptism, Transfiguration, and Resurrection of Jesus. These would have been even more revealing about the Spirit had there been a scientific understanding when the revelation was developing. What our ancestors conveyed about their understandings of God were au courant with the knowledge of reality available to them at the time as we have to be about what is now accessible to us. A continuing and fresh appropriation of reality keeps and makes for renewed concepts rather than merely a reiteration of former ones.

An example of updating can be found in John Zizioulas's understanding of person. He sees it as constitutively relational. Thus in contrast to a boundaried understanding of personhood as an individuated self, thus static rather than open, personhood must be seen as "even ek-static, ever in movement towards communion," thus always transcending "the boundaries of the self" and free to do and be so (*Communion and Otherness* [T. & T. Clark, 2006], 213).

A person's uniqueness, therefore, "is established in communion." This is what makes each person "unrepeatable," someone who forms part of a relational existence which is indispensable and irreplaceable (214). Behind the evolution of the meaning of personhood is the fourth-century Cappadocian understanding of the Persons of the Trinity as "hypostatic," i.e., ecstatic *mit gusto*. The Trinity is constituted of Persons whose being is relational as is ours.

November 24

I'm still thinking about Appropriation. A laziness has developed because the category of "appropriation" has generally been neglected or overlooked by Christians about the Trinity. Since the Trinity is One, it is too easy to speak of the One God at work in all that God has made as if God was undifferentiatedly one Person, doing one thing, acting one way. While the oneness of God remains true, the threeness of the one God is equally true. There is a proper role for each of the Divine Persons. The neglected or misunderstood category is attribution. Its neglect forgets the unique role of each of the Trinitarian Persons in creation.

So, to be more specific, the Spirit has a unique role in the life of what lives. It is one of the three sources of the uniqueness of the life of every living thing. To call the Spirit "life giver" does not exclude the fact of the role of the Source of the Origin of Life, Father, if you will. Nor does it exclude the belief that it is *through* the Son (Col. 1:15–20) that all things living and nonliving are made. What needs to be said and seen and believed is that the role of the Spirit is to be immanent in this interaction. The Spirit is the immanent Life-Giver. The Spirit is poured out, pours "itself" out, with something specific "in mind" in doing so, that is, that the living thing poured into both become itself and in turn come to be one with the communion-of-Persons that the Trinity is. The bestowal of the Spirit on the *creata* does not cancel Its real relation of communion in the Trinity.

Again, the stuff God makes makes itself with the help of the Spirit. The mind of the Spirit as also that of God who is the font of life, and of the Son through whom all things come to be is that each should reach the fullness of its potential and thus come into eternal communion with the Three. This scenario does not ignore the fact of suffering. On the contrary, suffering is a frequent purifying experience of living things freeing them from pathogens. Or better—making them smoother stones in the wall of living stones that makes for pure worship in the temple of God.

The communion of saints includes the things whose living glorifies God and whose expiration gives a permanence to their doing so. "His eye is on the sparrow and I know he watches me" (Luke 12:6). "If God's being is communion, then this means that creatures are able to be and to become because of their life-giving relationship with the Persons-in-Communion" (Denis Edwards, *Breath of Life* [Orbis Books, 2004], 125). What is distinctive about humans among the living are their capacities for knowing and choosing and being conscious mediators between all living things and God. In this sense, *Homo sapiens*'s uniqueness is to be a priestly species.

November 25

Information has superseded *being* in some people's repertoire as the fundamental, ontological building block of reality. They come to this because it is not learned that the most elemental form of biology has developed from what has been stored in the macromolecules of DNA. These contain codes which instruct the formation of proteins. The proteins themselves have causal effects on the genes, but the genes also have their own minds as it were, and from them something very specific happens. The genes instruct; it is as if they are intentional, "not in the mental sense but in the sense of seeking desirable outcomes" (Paul Davies and Neils Gregersen, eds., *Information and the Nature of Reality* [Cambridge, 2010], 337; Gregersen's chapter titled "God, Matter, and Information").

We now realize that genes are a complex hierarchy in which some genes regulate the activity of other genes or send signals to them (136). But sending signals entails or implies the transmission of information. Information as used in biology is "only for causes that have the property of intentionality" (John Maynard Smith, "The Concept of Information in Biology," in *Information*, ed. Davies and Gregersen, 139). It is becoming clear to biologists that there is a complex hierarchy of regulatory genes that send signals that are essentially symbolic or semantic or biosemiotic (142).

A cell "interprets" its environment according to its interests. These interests and habits of a cell's conduct, like that of the organism itself of which the cells are the basic unit, has a history, usually long and intertwined with evolutionary history itself (337). Gregersen speaks of an "information of connectivity, i.e., of absorbing and bringing into resonance a given situation with the interest of biological systems from cells to organisms" (338). Again, notice the respect the Spirit as Connector accords to the most minute processes in each living thing while pursuing its role as immanent Lord in the development of the ever-emerging whole.

November 29

"That all may be one" (John 17:20). This is what was in Jesus' heart, according to John, before his last supper was over and before he went from the meal scene to be arrested. It would be good to dwell on this one-ing "thing" because people have the capacities to be one makers, making wholes out of parts. Whether in our lives or in our work whole-making is how we go about making sense of our lives.

We should ask ourselves: For whom is this whole-making being done? And further, what larger whole is one contributing to in making or bringing about wholes? The usual way we do this is by doing justice to the pieces of reality we are apprised of in our immediate circumstances. Data affect our consciousness disassembled, and we seek to assemble them and make them and ourselves a little more coherent. We are descendants of Adam in doing this; it is natural to us. But as Christians, we seek to go beyond the wholes we are making to the one-ness that Christ came and died and rose to affect and effect.

Both humans and Christians weave oneness up from below, so to speak, stitch by stitch, day by day, one moment in personal relation with the next in personal relation. The mission of God in Christ is this one-ing thing that is going on now in history and is being done even now though not evidently and not well and needing constant assistance with the forbearance and forgiveness of God.

The relationship between God and nature gains insight by looking again at Jesus. He was a unique entanglement of nature and grace. The faith-filled writings about him are not always the best way to catch a glimpse of this connection, since they tend to be written for our edification about him and God. This makes information about his oneness with nature more difficult to come by. This comment does not question the inspired insights of the writers. His present status as "seated at the right hand of God" is not in question, though the place of matter in his life now is unclear.

Another interest that surfaces about matter is its relation to time. I have found much to ruminate about from the Gideon Goosen book *Space-time and Theology in Dialogue* (Marquette University Press, 2008). "A theology of space-time must include knowledge of kairos and chronos, eternal time, and synchronicity" (162).

Some of the history we need to give hospitality to is past ideas about time: Time (*chronos* in the Greek) is linear; its contents are about duration. Plato's idea about how to think about time was via the myth of the Demiurge, which posited that time is simply eternity moving.

Augustine also dealt with time from within his own experience of it. He had two very different experiences of it; the first was when his soul mate died and he became despairing. The second was when his mother died, and he sees time in light of her afterlife and its promise for human beings.

Martin Heidegger (1889–1976) presented ideas in *Being and Time* (New York: Harper and Row) that are very complex. He uses the word *time* in different ways, not one. They all rely on his ideas about *Dasein*. *Dasein* for him means that the individual is always projecting the self beyond itself within time. If we didn't, time wouldn't mean much. So he has a subjective view of time like Kant before him did. At the same time, all persons have to function within what he called "modes of temporality."

In three more recent authors eternity has different meanings. One is that it is unlimited, hence endless time. This meaning has its roots in the Hebrew Bible. For Barth "eternity has and is the duration which is lacking to time; it has and is simultaneity" (Hunsinger, ed., *For the Sake of the World: Karl*

Barth and the Future of Ecclesial Theology [Wm. B. Eerdmans Publishing, 2004],193).

The second meaning of eternity is timelessness. It is without time. Past and future are eliminated. Another view is Oscar Cullmann's, who differentiates the present age from the age to come. This is dualistic. A third view is Rahner's. It has to do with freedom and with the coming in the course of time to the fullness of our humanity when our freedom is freely used for coming to this fullness. So there's been on the one hand an over-identification of time and eternity as well as a complete separation between the two; these are both extreme. Better is some kind of interpenetration between these two.

A theology of time has been best begun by Rahner. He sees an interpenetration of time with freedom and with our experience of freedom. In a sense we begin to create an eternity depending on how we use time. Maybe the decision to marry is the best example of this. A choice which becomes past as soon as it is enacted can determine the subsequent situation within which one lives maybe even *usque in aeternum* (as the Mormon theology of marriage thinks). The self has plowed a furrow into the space or soil of its future. One then will have to proceed into the future from this past decision. So with that example, one can see that we are the primary agents of our relation to time and maybe even of eternity.

Some afterthoughts about time: In the course of writing this I got very hungry and kept watching the clock waiting for the noon hour when the cafeteria opens. As they say "a watched pot never boils." But then I found myself pursuing an idea and found that "time flies" and with that, hunger flees. And further experiences of one's "body clock" being on a different timeline when one flies internationally than that of the time of the place one lands. A final distraction about time is the sly adage "time is money" or the timeline of "billable hours." All of these comments reinforce the factor of subjectivity in this time matter.

Apart from revelation, most information comes from what has been and is still being communicated to us and in turn appropriated by us, whether from parents or from education in general, not to mention through our senses and from the stories of which we are a part, as well as from the various bodies of knowledge like the sciences. The information that is revelational differs from the other kinds of information because of its authority and the transcendental scope of the kind of knowledge it conveys.

How does revelational information differ from other information and how does it fit into or disconnect from other kinds of knowledge? It is knowledge born of faith both in the contents conveyed as well as in what is believed to be the source of this knowledge.

One of the pluses of the biological character of information is that it will move us, I believe, beyond classical metaphysics as we have known it. Maybe then the character of the Logos before Jesus' incarnation can resurface.

All information invites reception. It isn't information until it is appropriated and informs. Its reception depends on its trustworthiness as information. All information comes through the sieve of interpretation, which is usually multilayered. If the information that is considered revelation is received by believers, it becomes a profound source of meaning, their own meaning and of everything and everyone else's.

When did this phenomenon of information as revelation begin? Archaeology, paleontology, and early anthropology would say it was from the beginning of hominids and in turn of *Homo sapiens*. Our "primitive" ancestors experienced God as revealing a godself and they themselves as being communicated to by this communicator, though the variation in the number of images of what this information was and who this source was (and is) boggles the mind. The fact of their believing that they were privy to revealed knowledge is the constant in the matter. This revealed knowledge led to ways and words and deeds that are traceable without these necessarily including thematic reflection on the beliefs and religions of the recipients of this information, that is, theology. Although we are covering an enormous time span by these assertions, it appears that some of the other constants in the responses of our forebears to revelation as they appropriated it were awe, guilt, worship, fear, hope, virtue, power, and call. Their "sacred" stories, which convey this information, indicate that openness to the transhuman is inherent in being human. The most important information that can inform us always entails believing to some degree.

What is understood theologically today as opposed to yesterday about the information that claims the status of revelation? That it is misleading to spatially locate it coming from a transcendent (above) source, as opposed to an immanent (below) category. Biological information theory considerably blurs this line of beyond versus within. So does our experience of the divine as communicating to us in, through, and with nature.

I end this diary with an image, the difference between nothing and the Spirit. Wayne Gefter and his daughter Amanda have decided that the source of everything is nothing. Since "a thing is defined by its boundaries," they define nothing as a state of infinite unbounded or boundary-less homogeneity (Amanda Gefter, *Trespassing on Einstein's Lawn* [Bantam Books, 2014]). This book would put Spirit where they put nothing. The unboundaried love of God making stuff and accompanying it as it makes itself—this is how I see Spirit as not only the source of everything but of our meaning and of all boundaried things, too.

Index